HOW TO STOP BULLYING

D0995603

By the same author

How to be a People Person
Take Charge of Your Future

Uniform with this book

HOW TO STOP BULLYING

POSITIVE STEPS TO PROTECT CHILDREN IN YOUR CARE

Márianna Csóti

Author of *How to be a People Person* **and**
Take Charge of Your Future

RIGHT WAY

Constable & Robinson Ltd
3 The Lanchesters
162 Fulham Palace Road
London W6 9ER
www.right-way.co.uk
www.constablerobinson.com

This edition published by Right Way,
an imprint of Constable & Robinson, 2008

A copy of the British Library Cataloguing in Publication
Data is available from the British Library

ISBN: 978-0-7160-2187-2

Printed and bound in the EU

1 3 5 7 9 10 8 6 4 2

For all children – may they learn to value humanity

I should like to thank:
Dr Gill Salmon, Consultant Child and
Adolescent Psychiatrist, for her invaluable help
with this book; it is much appreciated;
and everyone who contributed their stories.

For books on social skills training, assertiveness training and
raising empathy in children, and links to organisations that
help with bullying issues, go to *www.mariannacsoti.co.uk*

CONTENTS

INTRODUCTION

According to Bully OnLine, at least 16 children in the UK kill themselves each year because they are being bullied at school and no one in authority is doing anything about it. ChildLine has reported that four out of every five bullied children have asked for help and have done so repeatedly, despite fears of reprisal: many of ChildLine's calls are from young people who are still being bullied even after telling an adult.

How to Stop Bullying demystifies the issues of bullying, showing how parents and teachers can help prevent children from becoming, and being, victims, and from becoming, and being, bullies. The book also explains what bystanders can do to help stop bullying. Bullying may exist in today's life but we can do something about it: we each need to take responsibility for our own behaviour and the reporting of, and dealing with, undesirable behaviour in others.

The terms bullies and victims are transitory: a bully can stop being a bully at any moment as can a victim stop being a victim. The only reason these descriptions are used in the book is to identify behaviour at a particular time and they in no way label a child inherently as either a bully or a victim.

1

WHAT IS BULLYING AND WHAT DOES IT INVOLVE?

Before we can work to stop bullying, we need to understand what it is and why children do it. Knowing what bullying involves helps us identify it more quickly and makes it easier to explain to the perpetrators why their behaviour is unacceptable.

What is bullying?

Bullying in children is repeated aggressive behaviour – be it physical or emotional – by a child, or a group of children, usually aimed at a single child. It involves an abusive use of imbalance of power to cause oppression, and often fear, in the victim who finds it difficult to defend himself while the bully often derives pleasure from the situation.

Some definitions of bullying might also say that it is a deliberate – perhaps unprovoked – act. However, some victims, known as 'provocative victims', encourage, indeed almost incite, other children to pick on them. There are also the bullies who do not realise that their behaviour is bullying. They unintentionally bully because of a lack of awareness: of their actions and of the consequences and of how other people react because of their behaviour. Children may also lack impulse control – being unaware of the responsibility they have over controlling their emotions, particularly anger.

Physical bullying

Physical bullying – also classed as direct bullying as the harm is aimed directly from the bully to the victim – includes tripping up, pushing, punching, kicking; taking possessions and damaging them; threatening – forcing a child to do unsafe things such as in 'dares', and extortion; and preventing a child leaving a room, such as the toilets.

Non-physical bullying

Non-physical bullying is more common than physical bullying and has sub-groups which include both direct bullying, such as calling someone names to his face, and indirect bullying, such as spreading unkind rumours. Indirect bullying is harder for you and your child's teachers to spot – and for children to prove – and so is less likely to be stopped.

Provocative behaviour includes wearing racist badges or insignia, making rude or threatening gestures and pulling faces.

Verbal bullying includes name-calling; making racist, sexist and homophobic comments; making fun; being repeatedly critical; prolonged unkind teasing and making threats.

Relational bullying is the deliberate harming of peer relationships. It includes spreading rumours, gossiping, shunning, befriending and then not keeping confidences, deliberate splitting up of friendships to isolate a child and stealing a best friend.

Sexual harassment involves uninvited and unwanted sexual attention of any kind including sexual innuendoes, jokes, comments on someone's appearance, a spread of sex-related gossip and offensive 'sex' talk in the person's hearing. More commonly sexual harassment is carried out by boys on girls – or by male teachers on girls. But pupils also commonly sexually harass teachers of both sexes.

Cyber bullying – using modern electronic devices such as computers and mobile phones – has made bullying easier and is on the increase, especially by girl bullies. It includes bullies sending victims cruel or threatening emails, instant messages, chat room messages, and text messages; making threatening phone calls and leaving malicious phone messages.

It also includes making cruel comments about a child to other children in text or instant messages, in emails or in chat rooms, taking revealing photos with a mobile phone and sending them on to other children – or uploading them onto a website dedicated to making the subject of the photo's life a misery. Bullies can also use camera phones to make video clips of children being bullied or hit – commonly known as 'happy slapping' – and sending them to other children or uploading them to websites.

Cyber bullying is particularly malevolent as it doesn't end when school ends – it continues into the evening and over weekends reaching victims at home when they should be able to relax and feel safe.

Traits of bullies

Any child can become a bully – some children may not realise their behaviour is classed as bullying and stop when they are challenged or are informed of the hurt they are causing.

But some children are persistent or serial bullies, having bullied more than one child – and probably in a variety of ways. Since negative patterns of behaviour have evolved over a long period of time and have become widespread, it will take time to correct their behaviour. Efforts have been made to classify the personality traits a serial bully has.

Serial bullying

Having a need to control and to dominate other children. Very often bullies are seen as leaders of gangs or friendship groups. They often bully children outside their social group but can also bully from within, especially to defend their leadership status. For example, if a child from within the group has too many independent ideas, or suggests ideas in conflict with the leader, the leader might isolate the challenging child from the group, spread rumours, divulge secrets or tell lies about him.

Or the leader might feel challenged by a new child in the class having a sudden rise in popularity, threatening the leader's popularity – or friends from the leader's clique may want to defect and be this new child's friend too. To retain leadership status, the leader has to put a stop to that.

Leaders of cliques can also demand loyalty such as by asking other group members to lie for them to cover up wrongdoings. The members know that if they don't do as they are asked, they risk forfeiting membership of the group. The fear of isolation may be so intense that group members are prepared to do what's asked of them.

Some children are strongly attention-seeking – they don't value other people's thoughts and, should the conversation diverge from them, they will always interrupt to pull it back: 'Oh, I did that last year. It was great fun. We . . .'

Acacia had money and attention lavished on her. She was given ballet, singing and drama lessons. Her parents and extended family members told her how wonderful she was and how much better she was than the other girls. Blind to mistakes Acacia made and blind to the bullying of her younger siblings, her parents failed to discipline her or to teach her that she was not the only family member with worth – and that people outside the family had worth too.

Unable to stand any other child being in the limelight, Acacia bullied girls who were praised above her by spreading rumours about them and sending malicious text messages. Acacia chose to spend time with less talented and attractive girls so that she would always be the 'best' among them. One of these girls was so grateful to be included in the group that she would do whatever Acacia asked.

To gain attention, Acacia would over-dramatise any event for maximum effect. When a teacher accused her of bullying, Acacia burst into tears and exclaimed how the other girl had been making her life hell and that this was just another ploy by this other girl to get at her. Acacia was unable to accept responsibility for her own behaviour.

When it became clear that she would never be the success her parents had predicted, Acacia became antisocial, dropping out of school, becoming promiscuous and misusing drugs and alcohol. At age 17, she became pregnant and left home.

Being defiant and disliking rules. Children who bully can

be particularly aggressive towards adults in authority. However, not all bullies use open aggression – many choose to use manipulation instead. Children who use manipulation are thought to have better social skills than children who use overt aggression as they are good at predicting what other children are thinking and so can identify emotional weaknesses – and use the information to hurt their victim.

When bullies flout rules, they like their friends to flout them too – be it smoking in school, truanting or extorting money from vulnerable children. If friends don't want to do what's expected of them, they are called 'chicken'.

Being disaffected with school or being unhappy at school – children who bully may not feel connected to the school and many bullies feel depressed.

Becoming impatient and angry very quickly. Young petulant children who bully can throw a wobbly the moment they don't get their own way. Their sudden mood changes make them even more intimidating and other children will fear crossing them. Children with high levels of anger are likely to see aggression as justifiable.

Behaving impulsively can make children who bully very dangerous. Unpredictable behaviour is far more frightening than reasoned, logical behaviour.

Being fairly confident. To pick on victims successfully, bullies have to be sure of the outcome. However, those who physically bully may lack confidence in using non-violent strategies.

Having high, low or average self-esteem – there is no definite rule about this. Children who do bully because they have low self-esteem may be directing anger, for example, from parental rejection or from being bullied by children who are stronger in some way onto children who are more vulnerable than they are.

Some children may only have high self-esteem because the power and social dominance they experience when they bully gives them these positive feelings; so there is the risk that, when they are prevented from bullying, their self-esteem will plummet.

Being considered fairly popular, having a few close friends or 'supporters' and a few children who are less close but keen to be connected to the bully. Children who bully can be popular with adults too. In fact, they can be so charming that they frequently get rewarded with admiration and praise. They only show the nastier side to their nature in private which means that they get away with being bullies for longer: 'Alison? There must be some mistake. She's such a *nice* girl . . .'

Being good at making up plausible excuses for scenes witnessed or complaints made against them, making it hard to pin trouble on them. This can prolong unmasking a bully's identity. Some bullies won't accept their failings and instead project their shortcomings onto other people and blame them instead: 'He made me do it,' and, 'It's your fault I hit you. You shouldn't have made me so angry.'

Not liking teamwork or having to work jointly with someone or to share or discuss ideas or to ask other people's opinions on something.

Being low in empathy – being unable to understand life and emotions from another child's perspective.

What makes a bully?

The reasons for bullying are not straightforward. People are diverse; an individual's behaviour under certain circumstances is not necessarily the same as another person's behaviour. There are many factors involved.

Children from deprived backgrounds may be more likely to bully as they experience problems at home such as abuse, unemployment, divorce, imprisonment, violence, alcoholism and bereavement. They may be modelling their behaviour on the way their parents have brought them up or treat each other – studies indicate that children become more aggressive if they witness violence from their fathers directed at their mothers.

Some children might have not had effective parenting – where threats for discipline were made but not carried out, or carried out violently or where they were given little discipline and had become used to getting their own way and so won't put up with anyone crossing them.

Children from privileged backgrounds might bully because of the way they are encouraged to treat other people. I have known some children from private schools to be scathing and derisive of others – they said everyone made fun of everyone else. Even the teachers in assembly made fun of the children, including teasing someone because of his race. When I said this was racist, the children said it was not because the boy who was Asian joined in with the teasing and made fun of other people from his own ethnic group. I wonder how that boy really felt.

As a houseparent, I also came across cases of bullying and stealing by children from extremely wealthy backgrounds – and only with overwhelming evidence did their parents accept that their children behaved like this: 'I can't believe it of her. She's so gentle. She's never done anything like this before . . .' and, 'I don't know what made him do that. It's not really what he's like. Something must have upset him . . .' Yet it had taken a long time for suspicions regarding several occasions to produce actual hard evidence for one occasion – and for students to dare to admit to what was going on and to be prepared to be named. Deluded parents helped these bullies get away with it. And parents who are unsupportive of teachers, protecting their child at all costs, help their child bully again.

Children who are not treated equally in their families are more likely to bully – and more likely to have little respect for their parents.

Some children who bully may not know how to handle negative feelings of anger and frustration without resorting to violence and threats as they have not had a positive role model to learn from. Or they may act aggressively to get attention, other methods having failed.

Some children bully because they have an impulsive temperament – they act without considering the consequences.

Some children bully because they have been bullied – by adults or by other children.

Some children bully because they are jealous of others who are richer, have more friends or greater talent than themselves. Nearly 20 per cent of children who call ChildLine about bullying say their current tormentor was a former friend –

perhaps former friends are jealous they are no longer friends?

Some children bully just because they can and no one stops them. They may be bigger, stronger, older, more popular or more experienced in some way than the victim. They may enjoy humiliating others; bullying can entertain them when they are bored or disaffected with school.

Some children become involved in gangs and bully for group approval. Gangs are groups that become involved in criminal activity. Although in the past gangs were thought of as a boy's domain there are ever increasing numbers of girl gangs or girls being included in boy gangs.

Girls are becoming increasingly violent too; sometimes their violence exceeds that of boys as though they want to prove that they can be tougher than the opposite sex. Some of the things gang members are more likely to get involved with, apart from bullying, are stealing, burgling, vandalism, joyriding, drug and alcohol misuse and promiscuity.

Very often children join gangs because they don't feel they belong anywhere else and on their own can feel very impotent, especially if they feel they have no worth in their own family.

2

VICTIMS AND SIGNS
OF BULLYING

Since most victims try to hide the fact that they are being bullied, it is up to us as interested adults to spot the danger signs. This can be by recognising characteristics that are known to attract bullies – and so helping children become less of an easy target – and in noticing children's changed behaviour that signals bullying is taking place.

Signs of being bullied
A sudden change in your child's behaviour can mean she is being victimised. Look out for the common warning signs described below.

Being afraid to go out alone or at all – your child might worry about meeting the bullies and getting more of what's already happened or what the bullies have threatened will happen. He might feign illness and say he doesn't want to go to school; in extreme cases this can lead to a fear of attending school and result in 'school phobia'. Symptoms include: stomach aches, headaches, nausea, vomiting, frequent visits to the loo, crying, shaking and panic.

Having nightmares or being afraid to go to sleep. Your child might become depressed and even talk about harming herself.

Getting into trouble at school – if your child was previously well behaved, consider whether the trouble he is in now might be because he was forced to do certain things. Ask why he did those things, especially if this kind of behaviour is out of character, before blaming and getting angry with him. Be suspicious of inadequate or unlikely excuses.

Looking afraid all the time. Your child might look as though she is going to get into trouble – even when she has apparently done nothing wrong. She might start to stammer when you talk to her or avoid meeting your eyes. Reassure your child to encourage her to be open with you.

Asking detailed questions. Your child might suddenly ask you about topics in which he previously showed little or no interest or spend time wanting to fine-tune his understanding of a particular point. In Year 4, Geraint asked his mother about the facts of life. He then explained that he'd been laughed at because he hadn't correctly answered questions posed by boys at school.

Having missing or copied homework, or having poor concentration in class. Your child might have had her homework destroyed or forcibly lent out and copied – or teachers might report that your child's standard of work and concentration in class have suddenly dropped.

Having missing, torn or dirtied clothes. Your child might have been pulled to the ground. Watch out for him suddenly wanting to do his own washing to hide the evidence. PE kits and school books and mobile phones might mysteriously disappear without your child being able to account for how these things happened.

Stealing money or household food or goods. Your child might have to find money to pay bullies who have threatened her or to replace stolen dinner money so that she can buy lunch. She might be bribing bullies for her protection. Madeleine, in primary school, stole chocolate biscuits from home to give to children who, at one time, had bullied her. She ate none herself.

Coming home extremely hungry. If your child arrives home from school needing to eat large amounts of food, he might not have had any lunch. His dinner money might have been stolen, or his packed lunch might have been taken and rendered inedible – or he might be too embarrassed to eat in school.

When Natsuki came home from school she ate vast quantities straight away yet claimed she had eaten her packed lunch. But three years later, Natsuki admitted that she hadn't been eating her lunch. At first, friends in her class watched her and commented on what she ate. If she was eating sweets, or more sandwiches than they ate, they said she'd get fat. So Natsuki began eating her lunch in secret. Then her friends suspected she hadn't eaten at all and called her anorexic and kept close to her at break times. So Natsuki stopped having lunch altogether because she felt their gaze always on her. As a knock-on effect, Natsuki also avoided having other people see her eat. When her parents had guests to dinner she asked to eat in her room.

Having unexplained injuries – including bruises and scratches. Even if your child says he fell over or got tackled in rugby, he could be being bullied.

Changing travel times and routes to get to and from school. Your child might be being bullied between home and school, finding safety in unpredictability.

Having a sudden change in friends – or having no friends at all, or friends suddenly stopping coming round; your child might have been isolated.

Being upset by phone calls or text messages or trying to hide the computer screen. Your child might be being cyber bullied.

Personal labelling in a negative way. If your child is called useless and stupid by bullies and is given other negative labels, he might believe that these descriptions are true and start using the labels on himself.

Anything else that is suspicious should alert your attention. For example, if your child is stressed she might stop eating, over-eat or she might bully younger siblings.

Who are the victims?
Anyone can get bullied. It is often a matter of chance. Luke was leaving school with hundreds of other children. A girl with her older sister asked him to move out of the way so that

she could get by but because his way was blocked he said, 'No.' Immediately, the older girl said, 'Do you want to pick a fight?' The caretaker heard and separated them. Luke hung back to let them get ahead but he didn't wait long enough. As he overtook them, the girls recognised him and physically attacked him.

Alfie threw an orange across the classroom to a friend. But it missed his friend and hit the class bully, Dan. Although it only brushed Dan's pocket, he got up and told Alfie, 'You're dead.' Whenever Dan saw Alfie, Dan spat at Alfie and repeated the threat.

Although some bullying can be just because of being in the wrong place at the wrong time or from an accident as in the above cases, bullies can pick on anything about their victim that is different. This can be due to many factors including their race, religion, culture, sexuality, the way they speak, what they eat and the clothes they wear. Or it can be over having differences in their, or their parents', lifestyles.

When I was teaching, a boy goaded a girl for the entire lesson – although I hadn't heard the whispers. Suddenly, the girl stood up, grabbed her chair and held it above the boy's head. I managed to take it from her before she hit the boy with it. I asked the girl to sit in the prep room under the supervision of the technician while I finished the lesson. Then I questioned both of them separately and found out that the boy had been calling her mum a slag. She was in tears. I believe her mother did have boyfriends but that was nothing to do with the boy – and I told him. I asked him to apologise to the girl – and told her she must never hurt anyone no matter what was said to her.

Some children are bullied because of their physical appearance. For example, they may be much shorter or taller than average or have freckles, or be an early or late developer during pubertal years. A study by Janssen and others (2004) in Canada of 11- to 16-year-olds showed that obese girls are 90 per cent more likely to be bullied than healthy-weight girls – and overweight and obese boys aged 15 to 16 are more likely to be bully/victims (children who both bully and are victims of other bullies) than boys of healthy weight.

Serial victimisation and victims' traits

Much bullying is not by chance, however, which is borne out by the fact that many children leave one school to escape bullying only to have it start up with a new set of bullies in the next school. Traits that have been found to increase the risk of victimisation are explored below.

Being timid. Victims tend to be shy and awkward in social situations, passive and lacking in competitive spirit, making it unlikely they will challenge bullies.

According to research by the young people's charity, Young Voice, over-controlling parents who do not allow their children to make their own decisions can make them more vulnerable to victimisation as they lack the self-confidence necessary to resist bullying. Experience of corporal punishment or experience of more aggressive violence in the home can make children more likely to become victims – as well as bullies.

Not being physically strong or co-ordinated – children can easily be a point of ridicule and are seen as unable to protect themselves.

Being anxious, depressed or without supportive friends shows victims as easy targets; they are more likely to internalise their problems and not seek help from other people.

Displaying certain behaviour has been found to invite bullying. This includes behaviour peculiar to a medical condition, crying for little reason, irritating other children, having unusual mannerisms or showing off, especially in crowded areas where there are more children to notice. Research by Olweus (1993) found that 'provocative' victims tend to be impulsive and show irritating and inappropriate social behaviour; they may also try to bully other children.

3

WHAT SCHOOLS CAN DO TO STOP BULLYING

A 'whole school approach' is widely recommended to combat bullying in schools which involves a large commitment from teaching and non-teaching staff and co-operation of pupils and parents. No single scheme is effective in stopping all bullying so a range of strategies needs to be developed, implemented and regularly appraised for effectiveness, adapting where necessary. Sharing ideas between schools can also be very productive. If you are concerned about the way your child's school handles bullying, use the information below to help you challenge the way the school is run.

Anti-bullying policies

By law, every school must have an anti-bullying policy. But they need to be strong documents, living and breathing in minds of staff and pupils – not pieces of paper that were written to satisfy current legislation and then filed away only to be pulled out at the next inspection.

Anti-bullying policies should be written in consultation with staff, parents, children and the local community in the light of the bullying carried out by pupils attending that particular school even if it does not actually happen on the school premises – which helps staff to come to their own definition of bullying – and in the light of the solutions that have been successful. The consequences of children telling about bullying should also be included. If people are consulted, they are more likely to have an interest in making sure the policy actually works and it will encourage them to uphold the values the school promotes. Staff, as well as pupils, should be protected by the anti-bullying policy. For example, staff should be protected by the school against sexual harassment and homophobic comments as well as against physical assaults.

Schools should keep records of bullying incidents so that patterns of bullying can emerge. Schools can use this information to adjust their anti-bullying policy to target bullying behaviour in areas of need.

Schools could send out anonymous questionnaires to children to tell whether the anti-bullying policy is working and if it is being correctly implemented. However, children need to be clear on what bullying is and isn't – for example, it is not bullying when two children equally matched for strength have an occasional spat. Examples of bullying could be included in the questionnaire.

Schools could use the Bully/Victim questionnaire and the software to process the data devised by Professor Dan Olweus of the University of Bergen, Norway. He also devised a comprehensive Bully Prevention Programme to reduce the incidence of bullying among primary and secondary schoolchildren.

By comparing past and present surveys, schools can tell how effective their measures are. If there is no clear improvement in the amount and severity of bullying, either the policy is at fault or staff members are not working together to provide the right environment for a social change in and around the school.

There could be a day's conference where teaching and non-teaching staff, educational psychologists and parents are brought together to become informed on aspects of bullying – including prejudice and stereotyping – and to suggest solutions if the anti-bullying policy is not working. The anti-bullying policy can be amended to take on board the things that have been said. By attending the conference, everyone should have the same aim in mind and be supportive of the methods agreed upon in making the anti-bullying policy more effective.

Schools should make their anti-bullying policy available on their website and on noticeboards so that parents can consult it in times of trouble and also be aware, and make their children aware, of the help and support on offer.

Clear sanctions for children who do not stop bullying should be laid out in the anti-bullying policy. They could start with removal from the class or group, being kept away from other children during lunch and break times, preventing children from going on non-educational school trips, preventing children from attending rugby or football practice.

Or a bully could be asked to write a story with her starring as the victim – or drawing a picture with her as the victim – to help raise empathy for her victim. Where a child has extorted money he should be made to repay that money – the school could give him a lunchtime job such as working in the canteen or an after-school job such as picking up litter or cleaning corridors and classrooms. Alternatively, the child's parents may be able to employ him at home.

Another common sanction is having after-school detention – but bullies could be given a compulsory programme with other bullies of anger management, learning positive social skills, learning assertiveness skills and in raising empathy for others. By showing that positive social behaviour is worthwhile, bullies might accept that it is a valuable leadership skill – and turn to influencing children through positive rather than negative means.

Victims could be offered something similar designed to help them make friends, increase their social skills and self-esteem and to teach them assertiveness skills. Some victims might also need to be taught anger management. Teachers and senior pupils could be trained to deliver such programmes.

If these sanctions and approaches have failed to stop the bullying, then bullying children should be suspended or even permanently excluded. Too often it is the victims who change schools to escape bullying and then the victims, their families and other children in the school see the bullying children as having won.

Written behavioural contracts could be introduced for bullies to sign, stating that they will not continue specific bullying behaviour. This gives the message that bullying has been taken seriously. The contract ought to include the sanctions the school would use should the contract be broken. The bullies' signature could be witnessed by a senior member of staff and by their parents. Schools could save time by using standard forms, so that they only need to insert the relevant details. Schools will need to follow up with bullies and victims to check that the bullying has stopped.

To punish or not to punish?

Many strategies to deal with bullying have been developed for use in schools. Those which do not focus on punishment are known as humanistic approaches; punishing bullies is considered to be dealing with aggression by using further aggression through an imbalance of power and has sometimes been found to increase bullies' aggression against their victims by their seeking revenge. Humanistic approaches aim to facilitate change in the way children think and behave so that they can get on peaceably – but there is no requirement to become friends.

Having a variety of strategies to draw upon allows schools to choose which is the most appropriate to fit the situation brought to their notice – and if one strategy has not been effective they can try another.

The No Blame Approach

Barbara Maines and George Robinson in the UK adapted the Swedish Farsta Method – developed by Karl Ljungström from a method outlined by Anatol Pikas – to become the seven step No Blame approach to use when a group of children has been bullying – or when one child bullies with her friends as witnesses. The approach assumes that the victim has not been provocative or involved in bullying too.

Step 1. 'Talk with the victim' to discuss his feelings, to invite him to produce a piece of writing or a picture to illustrate his feelings, to find out who was involved, to explain the way the approach works and to ask who he would like to make up the discussion group (in step 2) with the bullies. The victim is also invited to come back at any time if there is a continuing problem – and the teacher checks what information the victim has given that can be revealed to the group. Unlike in the Farsta Method the victim is not asked about how the bullying had been done, when and where it had been done and for how long it had been happening.

Step 2. 'Convene a meeting' with the bullies and a group of trustworthy children – to raise the social conscience of the group – in the absence of the victim but with the victim's knowledge and agreement.

Step 3. 'Explain the problem' using the victim's writing or picture to emphasise his distress and to explain why the teacher is worried about the child. Reasons why the bullying occurred are not explored.

Step 4. 'Share responsibility.' The group members may feel uncomfortable after being told the reason for the meeting. They are told no one will be punished; they have a combined responsibility to help the victim to be happy and safe and they are needed to help solve the problem.

Step 5. 'Ask the group members for their ideas.' Each group member makes a suggestion of how he or she can make the victim feel happier.

Step 6. 'Leave it up to them.' Give the group members the responsibility of righting the situation in the ways they'd described.

Step 7. 'Meet them again.' About a week later, the teacher discusses with each child separately, including the victim, how things have been going.

The No Blame approach does not advocate involving parents – but the Farsta Method does. Professor Dan Olweus contends that it is important to inform and involve parents – of bullies and victims – at an early stage of the preventive work. Most of us would argue that we have a right to be kept informed about all aspects of our children's behaviour and how they have been treated in school. And informing us of our child's aggressive or passive behaviour may help identify and remove any causative factors of which we become aware.

Michele Elliot, Director of Kidscape, a charity to help prevent bullying and child abuse, does not support the seven step No Blame approach since evidence she has been sent from parents suggests it does not work. However, what is not clear is whether these teachers were trained to use the approach and whether they checked it was successful.

In a primary school, Bethany was isolating Amber by telling other girls that if they played with Amber they were not allowed to go to the after-school club. Mrs X asked all the parents of the girls involved to come to school for a meeting. The parents of the children who had been coerced into not playing with Amber knew what the meeting was about. But the parents of the bullying children did not.

Mrs X talked in vague terms, insisting that no child should be named because of 'no blame, no shame' and spoke of how children should behave towards one another generally. The parents of the bullying children were bewildered, wondering what the meeting had been about. And the bullying continued. Clearly, Mrs X was not using Maines' No Blame approach.

Schools could vary their approach to improve efficacy once teachers have been trained in the essentials of a particular programme. Because of the controversy over people thinking that 'no blame' means no consequences, Barbara Maines and George Robinson have since changed the name to the '(No Blame) Support Group Method'.

The Method of Shared Concern

The Method of Shared Concern was devised by Anatol Pikas for working with bullying situations where a group of children is involved in bullying. It has four stages. Before the first stage, teachers gather information secretly about who might be involved and whether the victim could have somehow provoked any of the behaviour.

Stage 1. The bullies are interviewed separately, starting

with the main bully – for about ten minutes – in quick succession with no advance warning which prevents them deciding as a group what to say, reconstructing events to suit their purpose. It also makes each of them personally responsible for what he or she says – and what each did to the victim or didn't do to protect the victim; it 're-individualises' them.

The children are talked to calmly and without accusation to encourage them to be open and honest. The reasons for the bullying are not explored as it is considered to be time-consuming and children often do not know why they have bullied.

Open questions are used (the bully cannot give a simple yes or no to these) such as: 'I understand that you have been unkind to Amber. Tell me about it.' If the bully tries to blame the victim, the teacher ignores it and remains focused on the problem. If the bully won't answer, the teacher waits patiently until she does.

When the bully admits to being involved she is asked, 'What do you suggest can be done to help Amber?' If the bully thinks of a positive suggestion, she is praised for it. If a solution is not likely to be helpful, the bully is asked, 'What would happen if you did that?' If the bully can't think of possible solutions, the teacher suggests some: 'How do you think this idea might work…?'

Suggestions might include asking Amber to come to the after-school club and showing concern if she doesn't want to. The bully could tell Amber that she will look after her and that Amber will be safe. The bully could apologise for her behaviour – and even make Amber a card to say sorry. The bully could invite Amber to play with her and her friends at break times and share any treats she might have – or the bully could leave Amber to play with her friends while she played with some of her own.

If the bully shows no empathy with the victim, the teacher tries to increase empathy such as by asking, 'How do you think it feels to be left out by friends?' and, 'How do you think it feels to be told you can't join in with something all your friends are doing? How might Amber's friends feel being told that they have to choose between friendship and an after-school club?'

Each interview ends with the bully being asked to carry out her suggestions.

Stage 2. The victim is interviewed last to make bullies' revenge less likely: 'I hear there have been some problems lately. Can you tell me about them? How has this made you feel? What do you think can be done to improve the situation?' If the victim has provoked the bullying, or indeed taken part in bullying herself, the teacher can discuss ways in which the victim can change her behaviour. How the victim can strengthen other relationships can also be discussed.

Stage 3. A follow-up meeting with individuals reveals whether the situation has resolved and whether they have made a positive and genuine commitment to change. If they haven't, the teacher continues to work with the children – sometimes separately and sometimes with the bullies in one group and the victim on her own.

If the bullying has stopped, the teacher asks the children to continue doing what they have been doing and tells them there will be a group meeting in the future where the bullies must individually make a positive comment about the victim.

Stage 4. The teacher meets with the bullies first and discusses what they will say to the victim. The victim later joins them. If the victim was provocative, as well as hearing how the other children will behave towards her, and listening to the positive comments made about her, she must also make a commitment to change. The teacher praises all the children for their co-operation and for having managed to find solutions to the problem and work through them. The situation is reviewed again in six weeks' time with another meeting. The Method of Shared Concern does advocate informing parents.

The punitive approach
Punishing bullies is a traditional approach that is often used when other strategies fail or when bullying has been very serious. After bullying has been established by interviewing

all concerned, staff explain to the bullies why their behaviour is unacceptable – referring to the definition of bullying from the anti-bullying policy to prove it.

Bullies are told that their bullying behaviour must now stop but if it continues, or the bullies take revenge on the victim, they will be dealt with extremely harshly – in the manner described in the school's anti-bullying policy. This may ultimately lead to suspension or exclusion. If a victim is physically assaulted or stolen from, the police may be called. Parents are informed about what has happened and the steps the school intends to take. (Actual sanctions have been discussed in *Anti-bullying policies* above.)

Bully courts could be introduced. Selected pupils and staff listen to what has happened and decide what the consequences should be. This has been found to be successful by Michele Elliot, Kidscape Director. However, bully courts should not be used for trivial cases of bullying, which are considered to be easily resolved by teachers, or for very serious cases which are a matter for the police. The victim needs to agree to dealing with the matter in the bully court.

There is no audience in the bully court. Each child involved gives evidence and is questioned by the panel. The panel discusses the case in private and makes its judgment about what is to happen to the bullies who may appeal to the Headteacher if they disagree. A record is kept of all the proceedings and the verdicts to become precedents for future cases.

Peer support in schools

ChildLine in Partnerships (CHIPS) is an initiative run by ChildLine. It involves training children in primary and secondary schools to become buddies, known as Peer Supporters, focusing on the importance of children listening to one another – many children prefer talking to their peers as they don't feel comfortable talking to their parents or to their teachers.

In secondary schools, for example, Peer Supporters in Years 10 and 12 are trained to talk, listen, comfort and support children in need of help and advice, and to intervene if they see bullying behaviour – they wear a badge to identify themselves. They can run a drop-in centre at lunchtimes and take it in turns to be 'on duty'; their photos can be displayed on a notice board with the times they will be available. Peer Supporters can also be attached to a form in Years 7, 8 and 9 to have direct contact with children during registration periods.

As well as having the status of a Peer Supporter, these children gain from learning and practising new skills and can demonstrate that they are dependable and respected – things which can be mentioned on job and university applications. They can share their knowledge directly with their peers or share it through example; taking positive skills home can also benefit the family.

Children could be encouraged to befriend children outside their usual circle of friends. If pupils are on the look-out for children on their own they could 'mop them up' so that they won't be identified as friendless by bullies.

Older pupils could be asked to help younger pupils with their work. Children from Year 6 (or in some cases Year 7) in primary schools and Years 11 and 12 in secondary schools could regularly give help to raise the standard of children's work, protecting them from being made fun of and allowing them to achieve more for themselves.

Older children could be trained to run after-school workshops for younger children – such as on friendship and assertiveness skills. This could be a form of community service.

Sex and relationship education and homophobia

Every school should have a regularly reviewed policy for Sex and Relationship Education (SRE) containing a definition of SRE, a description of how SRE is provided and who is responsible for providing it, how SRE is monitored and evaluated and an explanation of parents' rights to withdraw their children from SRE lessons.

The *Sex and Relationship Education Guidance*, issued in

July 2000 by the Department for Education and Employment, makes it clear that teachers should 'deal honestly and sensitively with sexual orientation, answer appropriate questions and offer support.' But some teachers shy away from teaching about sexuality or are under the misapprehension that they are not allowed to discuss it with children. Fion's Year 9 class was told by the Personal Social and Health Education teacher that homosexual relationships could not be included in their list of relationship categories as she was not allowed to talk about them.

The Education Act of 1996, Section 28, regarding the prohibition of local authorities in England and Wales 'promoting' homosexuality, was legally obsolete with respect to teaching in schools. Section 28 has now been repealed so no longer has any bearing at all on decisions schools make regarding the content of SRE.

In the 2002 OFSTED report it is stated, 'In too many secondary schools homophobic attitudes among pupils often go unchallenged. The problem is compounded when derogatory terms about homosexuality are used in everyday language in school and their use passes unchallenged by staff.' Children's understanding of the homophobic words they use and the impact they have on the children at whom they are directed should be explored in class – the same can be said of racial comments and labels.

If schools do not teach about homosexuality, bisexuality, transsexuality (also known as transgender) and intersex, homophobic bullying will not be addressed. Children will continue blithely to use labels like 'gay', 'bent', 'sissy', 'dyke' and 'tranny' as universally derogative terms as well as attacking children for not being, or appearing not to be, heterosexual. Myths and prejudices children may hold about sexuality will be perpetuated and schools will fail to support children who know they are different but feel too ashamed to talk about it. Douglas and others (1998) found that 82 per cent of schools are aware of homophobic abuse, and 26 per cent of homophobic violence, but that only 6 per cent refer to homophobic bullying in their policies.

Rivers (2000) found that lesbian, gay and bisexual children are more likely to leave school at 16, despite achieving the equivalent of six GCSEs at grade C, that many have a regular history of absenteeism at school due to homophobic harassment and that 50 per cent contemplated self-harm or suicide – 40 per cent had made at least one attempt to self-harm.

It is thought that between 4 and 10 per cent of the population is lesbian, gay or bisexual – so a significant number of children in a school at any one time will be lesbian, gay or bisexual. So staff should not assume heterosexuality in one another, in their pupils or in their pupils' parents. Some children at school may have same sex parents.

Other ways schools can help

Having a clear leadership structure that supports the message that bullying is unacceptable is vital. Serious bullying should always be referred to a senior member of staff.

Having a strong ethos that promotes tolerance and respect, including respect for difference and diversity, increases children's trust for teachers so that they are more likely to seek help.

Ensuring good communication between staff, parents and children allows everyone involved in a child's well-being to be kept informed of any problems – bullying or otherwise.

Using parent-teacher meetings to inform parents about the steps the school is taking to combat bullying and to explain what methods are being used and how successful they are – and how parents can help – can be an effective way of communicating progress and needs.

Being swift to act whenever the issue of bullying comes up, and following it up to check it does not resume, gains victims' trust.

Dealing with bullies on an individual basis allows a fair and appropriate resolution. All children involved should be treated with understanding and personal and home problems should be taken into account.

Dealing with victims on an individual basis instils trust and respect. It involves listening to what they want – some children just want a listening ear or some advice and do not want intervention; some may want to try to handle the situation themselves with support.

Ensuring consistency in approach by all staff – teaching and non-teaching – reinforces the anti-bullying message. All staff members need to respond and act in the same way, take children's concerns into account when dealing with them and know to whom to report incidents of bullying and other bad behaviour.

Having clear standards of behaviour for staff as well as children reinforces the anti-bullying message by example. Staff and children should know that any form of sexual harassment is unacceptable. Staff should not make personal comments to children and they should stop children from using them on one another. The school should also have a clear policy on how it tackles swearing – as well as showing disrespect for others, swearing can be used as a tool for bullying.

Encouraging teachers to share vulnerabilities and experiences helps make the school an effective community and improves peer support and development. Working in isolation also leaves teachers vulnerable to stress-related illnesses; it can also mean that discipline is harder to maintain and so lessons are harder to teach.

Having mentors for new teachers helps guide and support them in effective classroom and school practices.

Ensuring that sufficient supervision is given at break times has been found to reduce bullying greatly. Low levels of supervision increase the risk of bullying.

Many children are afraid to use the school toilets as they fear getting trapped by bullies and don't feel safe going to the loo. In some schools, the doors hang off the hinges so can't be shut properly. Toilets should not be no-go areas for children.

Having lunchtime clubs helps to reduce the risk of bullying as vulnerable children can choose to join in supervised activities whilst having fun at the same time. Schools could provide a room supervised by, for example, non-teaching staff, for vulnerable children to go to. Games could be provided or children could bring their own. Children should also be supervised as they leave the premises at the end of the school day.

Having helpline numbers clearly visible in parts of the school gives victimised children access to adult help should they feel unable to confide to a teacher or to their parents. As well as having suggestion boxes for notes to be posted, secondary schools could also advertise a dedicated bullying email address so that children could secretly email their difficulties at any time. Research has shown that as children mature they are less likely to seek help directly from another person, preferring getting advice from helplines and the Internet.

Displaying anti-bullying posters that children themselves have made ensures that children feel involved and thereby committed to stopping bullying behaviour.

Removing offensive graffiti as soon as it is seen, and regularly checking toilets for graffiti, can help tackle homophobic and racist attitudes.

Avoiding sex-role stereotyping so that girls are not made fun of for being butch and boys are not made fun of for being camp is important in tackling homophobic bullying.

Avoiding showing favouritism to individuals or groups of children helps to decrease bullying due to jealousy. In Freya's school, two children from Year 6 were regularly asked to read in assembly – but no one else – and these children and their friends had regular special lessons with the Headteacher in the staff room and were given cakes to eat. They were targeted for bullying.

Avoiding too much emphasis on competitiveness at school helps prevent jealousy between children and decreases the bullying of teachers towards children. Gerard, who was having anxiety problems, was harangued by teachers in his private school to keep up with work as his GCSE grades would affect the school's position in the league tables. He was told that if he could not overcome his problems he might be asked to leave before he sat his external exams.

Being flexible regarding some school rules shows that the school is a caring school and encourages pupils to be caring too. For example, insisting children should not wear hats in school when they are bald from cancer treatment is blatantly unkind. One Headteacher even rang up a child's parents asking him not to attend school until his hair had re-grown – which did not allow other children in the school to learn acceptance and showed that the school was not prepared to protect the child from being bullied. What was more surprising was that the reason for his not having hair was not addressed – that he was at risk of dying. Was it fair to give the child an additional burden to deal with?

Dealing with children in non-aggressive ways encourages children to behave without aggression. This does not mean that if the teacher has to raise his voice to be heard above the hubbub that is wrong. For teachers, their voice is an invaluable tool. But what it does mean is matching their behaviour to what the children are doing.

When Gavin was about to strike Daniel with a plank of wood at the other end of the schoolyard, it was sensible for the teacher who saw this to yell at Gavin to stop as his voice would reach Gavin before he could. But when shouting is used for minor insignificant offences, it is aggressive. There is a saying that if you have a noisy teacher, you have a noisy class. To some extent my experiences back this up.

Banning camera phones in school – to avoid 'happy slapping' – and the use of other mobile phones in school time can reduce cyber bullying. It is unrealistic to ban phones altogether since many parents want their children to be able to contact them in the event of a change of plan in after-school activities or in an emergency. The proper use of mobile phones could be a matter of discussion among pupils.

Emphasising the fact that children cannot shift blame helps a child realise that everyone, even if acting as part of a group, is individually responsible for his own behaviour and that he is not absolved of an offence by saying someone made him do it.

Integrating anti-bullying issues into the school curriculum and highlighting them in assemblies, newsletters, student newspapers and on notice boards raises awareness of the unacceptability of bullying behaviour.

Openly valuing minority groups by having discussions about famous people in, for example, literature, history, science and maths, and by holding assemblies on different themes relating to prejudice, sexual harassment, sexuality and bullying helps reduce discriminatory behaviour among pupils.

Schools could also celebrate minority ethnic festivals such as the Hindu Festival of Light: Diwali, and the Jewish Festival of Light: Hanukkah. Dr Simon Hunter, from the University of Strathclyde, found that children who felt proud of their ethnic community coped best with bullying in terms of being more resilient to it and feeling less depressed, even among children as young as eight.

Having class discussions on behaviour and bullying actively involves every child in the school in bullying issues. Teachers in primary schools could use circle time and teachers in secondary schools could use free time during form periods – one day a week could be protected from assembly and administrative tasks – for Personal Social and Health Education or Citizenship lessons.

Children could be asked to come up with solutions to make their class a more rewarding one to be in. Suggestions might include having a few children nominated to remind other children to keep their behaviour within reasonable limits – but these children need to be taught how to do this assertively or they may behave towards aggression with further aggression. Having clear class rules can also help – such as not interrupting another child who is already speaking.

Subject classes that have problems could be invited to come up with their solutions. As well as promoting positive behaviour it helps children get on with people in a wider community – which is part of Citizenship.

Inviting current or past pupils to talk about their experiences of bullying can increase empathy pupils have for victims and show them that bullying is not a game; it is far more serious. Past pupils could talk about 'coming out' and the prejudices they may have encountered, urging the current school population to be more tolerant of differences.

Considering methods of keeping children safe from physical bullying will help look after children in the school's care and satisfy parents that the school is doing all it can. In Finland, some schools give wrist alarms, developed for the elderly, to known victims, who are at risk of physical bullying continuing, to summon help if they see their bullies approaching. When pressed, the button on the alarm sends a signal to a mobile phone – held by the teacher on duty. As a cheap alternative, victims could be given a Wrist-Mate Personal Alarm that sounds very loudly when pressed to alert staff.

4

WHAT TEACHERS CAN DO
TO STOP BULLYING

School should be a safe and supported environment that does not tolerate bullying at any level but tries to foster teamwork, acceptance and understanding among its pupils and staff. Here are some ways teachers could help schools achieve this.

General advice for teachers to stop bullying behaviour
Promote co-operation. Teachers could ask for help in carrying books or in handing them out, clearing away after practical work, and by asking children to help one another. Teachers could pair off children who don't normally work together and give them tasks to complete together.

Teach prosocial behaviour to ensure that the social skill level of the whole class is raised. This can be done formally by having lessons where social situations are discussed, and informally as certain situations arise. For example, if a child falls out with another child, the teacher could help the children settle their differences in non-aggressive ways and to apologise.

Praise all prosocial behaviour: co-operation, negotiation, compromise, conflict resolution and friendliness. In primary schools, teachers could give children stickers for prosocial behaviour. In secondary schools, teachers could give children special ink stamps in their homework books: when they have collected a certain number, they could be exchanged for a certificate.

Teach prosocial behaviour by example. This includes teachers being kind to children generally and not picking on timid children. Teachers should be ready to listen and show respect by not ridiculing wrong answers.

Ms Y separated Wanda in Year 8 to sit on her own in the lessons because she was talkative. One day Wanda was upset and passed a note to her best friend explaining what had happened in her family. The teacher took the note and read it out to the whole class in Wanda's presence in a deriding tone. She put on an affected voice, saying in mock sympathy, 'Ah.'

Ms Y could have read the note privately and later discussed with Wanda the inappropriateness of using lesson time to write it. Then she could have talked to Wanda about what was happening at home.

Some children have spotted senior teachers bullying newly qualified teachers; one pupil witnessed his female class teacher being sexually harassed by a male teacher – when this male teacher knew that the child was still in the classroom. If teachers are being bullied, how can the school stop the children from being bullied?

Intervene before a situation escalates – teachers can bring the conflict to a quicker conclusion which limits aggression between children. If the conflict arises during a lesson, the teacher could keep the children back at the end of the lesson to talk about what had happened and how each of them could contribute to putting it right.

Take heed of what children say and how they look – so that teachers can spot trouble and show caring towards their pupils. If a child has been crying or looks sad, teachers could ask what is wrong when they are alone together – a victim may brush off any troubles if publicly asked what the problem is.

Connect with pupils – teachers should show care generally towards children in the school. This will make it more likely that children will take on board what teachers say and for the children to care about their teachers and other children in the school. Connecting with pupils can have a positive spiralling effect in the same way that having a school full of angry, disillusioned teachers shouting throughout every lesson can have a negative effect.

Vary the seating plan of the class – particularly in primary schools – or have some activities where pupils are grouped randomly to increase the number of children each of them get to know. This can help new relationships to form and enables pupils to connect with many more children in the class.

Male teachers – and senior male pupils – should take a proactive role in stopping bullying behaviour by showing expectations of prosocial behaviour and by not using aggression when dealing with others. This can particularly help address the problem of aggressive boys.

Consider carefully the use of language in school – so that teachers help prevent children being permanently labelled. Much is made of 'Stop the Bully' posters and although this is a short and punchy message it doesn't allow for the fact that any child can show bullying behaviour and, when she doesn't bully, she may have many more apparent positive qualities. It may be more helpful for teachers to say, 'Stop Bullying Behaviour'.

Give children hope by taking their concerns seriously. Teachers should make sure that they listen to what children have to say and follow it up either personally or by referring the matter to a senior member of staff – and checking with the children that they are being given the help and support they need.

Emphasise commonalities. Bullies and victims may have more in common than either of them imagine. They probably enjoy listening to the same music, watching the same TV programmes, visiting the same websites on the net. They experience the same feelings when things go well or badly. They probably have similar fears, hopes and dreams. By breaking down perceived differences between children, teachers help them connect with one another.

Teachers should question their behaviour and their motives
It is often useful for teachers to 'observe' their own behaviour to help moderate their teaching performance since there are usually no other teachers to help them do this: most teacher/pupil interactions take place in isolation.

Criticism should be balanced or constructive when appraising a child's work to ensure that his self-esteem is not demolished: 'That's good; this needs a little more work . . .' and: 'It would be much better if you describe this person in more detail . . .'

Children should not be denigrated generally by teachers saying things like, 'Children weren't this naughty in my last school,' or, 'You are the laziest kids I've come across in my whole teaching career.' Neither should children be compared: 'Your brother wasn't like this – he worked hard.'

Children should not be made an example of unless what they have done truly deserves a public dressing down – and even then, it should be done in the context of the behaviour and not in passing at some other place in front of a new audience. For example, if a child was rude to another child during a lesson, the teacher could demand an apology for that child in front of the rest of the class who had heard the original insult. Or the teacher could say, 'That was totally out of order, Sylvia. I want to see you and the person you just insulted at the end of the lesson.'

Children should be given a chance to explain their side of things – and to have awkward conversations dealt with discreetly. Tamzeed was in the lunch queue when his English teacher, in front of all his friends and much of the rest of the school, shouted at him for not having handed in his homework. Tamzeed was normally quiet and hard-working therefore it was out of character for him not to have handed in his work on time. Had the teacher had a quiet word with him to ask what had happened he would have found out it was Tamzeed's first day back after his father had died.

Children should not be picked on unfairly by teachers as the imbalance of power is immense – and therefore the damage that can be done to that child and that child's education can be immense. A teacher, for example, calling a child stupid will have far-reaching consequences.

A more constructive way of dealing with a difficulty might be, for example, to praise the few times something is done well to balance necessary criticism and encourage more positive behaviour. Mico is usually late for the first lesson of the day. When he turns up on time, his teacher could either ignore the fact that Mico is punctual – but this does not reward him for the effort he has made. Or she could comment on it in a sarcastic way which punishes: 'Oh, Mico, what happened to get you out of bed this early?' Or she could give praise unencumbered by negative intent: 'Well done, Mico. You're on time.'

Equal positive and negative attention should be given to children regardless of gender, race, apparent sexuality, disability and personal likes and dislikes.

Positive attention includes asking a child a question and praising her if she gets it right, noticing an improvement in her work or behaviour, smiling at her, inviting her to answer in class, checking on the progress of her work during a lesson and offering praise or help.

Negative attention might be trying to trip up a child when teachers know he has not been paying attention – although this is fair if it is done equally to whoever might be daydreaming or distracted. Other negative attention includes ignoring a child's raised hand when the class is invited to answer a question and not checking on the progress of his work while checking on most other children's work.

If a class has equal numbers of boys and girls, equal numbers of boys and girls should be asked questions and given attention in class. The same applies for any other criterion of grouping. Some children like to dominate lessons with a barrage of questions – they can be told that they are not the only child in the class and that should there be more questions they can be answered at break time.

Ms Z was a Head of Department in a school that was, by far, predominantly white. A new girl called Mwangaza arrived in the class which was a top set. In her first lesson with Ms Z, Mwangaza was sent out for wearing trainers when other children had been previously admonished but not asked to leave the lesson. Just before the next lesson on another day, Ms Z saw Mwangaza outside the class and told her that she had been put down into the lower set for that subject. When

Ms Z was out of earshot the children in the class talked about Mwangaza – they felt convinced Ms Z's behaviour towards the black girl had been racist.

Whether there were justifiable reasons that the children could not know of, we can't tell. But the message that perhaps Mwangaza got – and definitely her ex-class mates got – was that she had been discriminated against. It would have been better had Ms Z asked to have a quiet word with Mwangaza and explained why she was moving her to a lower set. As it was, it looked as though Ms Z used her position of authority to remove a child from her class because of her race.

Several studies have shown that children of ethnic minorities have found fewer favourable interactions with their teachers and are more likely to be punished for offences that white children commit with little or no consequence. Black children, particularly boys, are more likely to be suspended from schools than white children for similar situations.

Children should not be punished for not conforming to gender stereotypes. For example, saying things to boys like, 'Don't be a such a wuss,' or, 'Don't be such a big girl's blouse,' or, 'What's this? The local knitting circle?' and, 'Are you lot having a mothers' meeting?' is a form of homophobic bullying regardless of the fact that teachers may have said these things in fun. Boys will be unable to accept the more sensitive side to their own nature and the nature of other boys if they are punished as soon as they exhibit some of that sensitivity or vulnerability – boys are notorious for finding it hard to express their feelings.

Teachers may punish girls for not conforming to gender stereotypes by upbraiding them for messy work – when boys with similarly disorganised work are let off the hook. Or they may show preference for attractive girls, smiling less and giving less attention to plain or tomboyish girls.

Hunter and others (2004) found that victimised girls perceive telling to be a more effective strategy, both in terms of stopping bullying and in helping them to deal with their emotions, than do boys. He suggests that future research should examine whether teachers treat boys and girls differently when they ask for help in dealing with aggression, as this may be one reason for their different evaluations of telling. For example, teachers may be more dismissive of boys' feelings than they are of girls' feelings.

Children should be given good reasons to trust and respect their teachers otherwise they will not be encouraged to go to them for help. Trust will be broken if teachers do not listen to what a child says and do not keep their promises or assurances. Respect is lost as soon as teachers do something that they tell children off for – for example, Ceri's teacher cheated by assisting some of his weaker classmates in the Key Stage 2 exam she was invigilating because the results affected the school's position in the national league tables.

Inform children about bullying

There are four groups of children involved in bullying. Those who perpetrate the bullying are the bullies, those at the receiving end of the bullying are the victims and those who witness the bullying are the bystanders. The fourth group includes those who both bully and are victims themselves: known as bully/victims. A study by Olweus (1978) found that approximately 20 per cent of victims also act as bullies.

Teachers could explain the different forms of bullying to children to ensure they know what it is and what they can do about it. They can also explain to children how bullying works and the roles involved in bullying so that they understand the very important role the bystander plays.

The process of bullying

The process of bullying, as described by Ken Rigby in his book, *New Perspectives on Bullying*, starts by a child, who sees himself as more powerful than other children, identifying a child who might be shy, anxious, isolated, an object of prejudice or physically less powerful. He then plans to hurt, undermine or humiliate the victim.

If the victim responds to victimisation by being disturbed or upset without challenging the bully, the bully feels gratified and may well be inclined to bully again. But what the bystanders do can affect the outcome; Salmivalli in Finland found the following roles in bystanders.

Outsiders do not take sides or become involved; they may walk away. But bullies see this behaviour as silent approval.

Reinforcers encourage the bullies' behaviour by laughing and showing approval.

Assistants join in and help the bullies.

Defenders try to comfort and help the victim and try to stop the bullying.

Research in Canada by Craig and others (1999) showed that 75 per cent of peer interventions were successful in stopping bullying. However, many bystanders don't stop bullying because of a 'diffusion of responsibility' among the crowd and because of fear of becoming the next victim. Some bystanders don't fully understand the process of bullying and worry they will make things worse for the victim or feel they don't have the knowledge or skills to intervene.

When the bystander does not take on the role of defender, but instead behaves as 'outsider', 'reinforcer' or 'assistant', the bully's empathy with, and sympathy for, the victim is reduced. So if no one steps in to stop the bully or to help the victim, thereby telling the bully that the victim is worthy of being defended, the bully will be encouraged to bully more. So the bully plans, over time, more and more elaborate ways of getting to his victim. With each bullying act, his empathy for the victim diminishes further. Bystanders, by taking up the defender role, play an essential part in stopping bullying.

If the victim ignores the bully, fights back, seeks help or appears not to be bothered by the bully's attempts – some children try to distract or amuse the bully to avert an attack – the bullying can either stop or the bully might think up different ways to get to the victim.

Sometimes, bullying starts in a very minor way in front of a teacher as a test. If the teacher does not react to support the victim, the bully is more likely to intensify the bullying. The bully responds in the same way if he knows that the victim has told a teacher but nothing happens as a result: the bully knows the victim has little or no support. However, if the teacher is seen to take the matter seriously, the bully may not try again.

Teachers should praise children for intervening or acting to stop bullying

Too often children don't like to interfere – they're not sure what to do or say. In a bullying situation, there is the added risk of the bully turning on them. So children need overt encouragement to speak out; they need to know that if they don't intervene, the bullying escalates and they need to find that, when they do tell, nothing bad happens to them. They should be praised for coming forward to protect either themselves or their friends.

However, some discussion might be needed about the difference of telling tales for minor misdemeanours and telling to protect themselves or their friends particularly in primary schools where much pettiness is evident. To help discussion, teachers could mention various scenarios and ask pupils to say whether it is something they should try to deal with themselves or something that is best for a teacher to sort out. Using examples that have recently come up in class makes it more relevant to the children.

For example, pettiness that does not need in the first instance to be passed to a teacher includes a child borrowing a school pencil from another table without permission – the children on that table could point out it is polite to ask first – and a child accidentally bumping into another in the school-yard – such a child would probably apologise and not find it funny if it is genuinely accidental.

A more serious situation that teachers should be told about is when a child belonging to a particular friendship group is not allowed to play with that group at break time. When Jessica told the teacher on duty that this was happening to her, the teacher was unsympathetic and told Jessica to find other children to play with. Jessica was excluded from playing with the children on her table for several days at a time on a regular basis and she stopped telling because she found that the teachers did not care. Eventually she learned not to trust the girls she sat with and made friends with other children in the class. The situation improved when the table sizes got bigger higher up in the school and Jessica sat with a larger group.

The teacher on duty could have acted the first time she was told about the situation by talking to the girls in the group, telling them it was unfair to exclude Jessica from their games. It might have prevented further unkind behaviour towards Jessica.

Classroom rules and teacher expectations

If teachers have clear rules, children will know where the boundaries lie and will be prepared to take the consequences if they knowingly cross them. Teachers need to ensure that the rules are kept and to understand that it is unfair to change rules at a whim or to keep reprimanding a child who has not broken a particular rule: these things could be considered to be bullying.

Teachers might like to think up a few key rules and then discuss with the class what rules they'd like to add – such as sharing equipment or other resources fairly and respecting one another. Involving the children will make it more likely that they will take more interest in keeping the rules and seeing that others in the class also keep them.

It will also help children respect the teacher if, when a teacher arrives late, an explanation and apology are offered – in the same way a teacher expects a child to offer an apology and explanation. And if a teacher has not marked work by the next lesson as is usual, an apology is also in order – teachers can only upbraid their pupils for handing in homework late if they, as a rule, do their 'homework' promptly too.

5

WHAT PARENTS CAN DO TO STOP BULLYING

By being informed about what bullying involves and how it affects children, parents are better able to help their children become less of a target of bullying, prevent their children from bullying – many children are bullies as well as victims – and to help when their child witnesses bullying.

How bullying affects your child's health

Understanding how bullying can affect your child's health will help you look out for warning signs – and help the professionals involved in your child's education take your concerns seriously.

Bullies commonly have ailments such as headaches, stomach aches, back aches, insomnia and feeling dizzy and they are more prone to feeling irritable, nervous, lonely and low. They are more likely to think about, and commit, suicide. Bullies are at increased risk of antisocial behaviour and for having negative attitudes towards school and education, resulting in underperformance and truanting.

In the long term, bullies tend to become aggressive adults who stand a much higher chance than average of obtaining multiple criminal convictions, especially for men who were aggressive as children. They are also more likely to be unemployed, abuse their spouse, and develop alcoholism, antisocial personality disorder, depression and anxiety.

Victims also suffer from minor ailments like bullies do but more frequently. They may also try to avoid school – and are more likely to have low academic achievement. Anxiety, low self-esteem, and depression are common; sometimes victims commit suicide. Being bullied can make victims view their peers as hostile, untrustworthy and having bad intentions leading to social anxiety and poor quality friendships. Internalising problems – not discussing them with people who can help – further isolates victims.

In the long term, victims may have difficulty forming any close intimate relationships, have difficulty trusting people, have low self-esteem and be prone to depression. Severely bullied young people can grow up to be angry and vengeful adults who are no longer willing to tolerate any kind of perceived oppression. Schäfer and others (2004) have found that victimisation at work is somewhat more common in former school victims.

Bully/victims have been found to be highly maladjusted – more so than children who are only victimised. In a study by Salmon and others (2000) being bullied was frequently a factor in presentation of adolescents to psychiatric outpatient services, with depression being in over 70 per cent of cases. In contrast, bullies and bully/victims were most likely to present with conduct disorders (see *Common conditions that coexist with ADHD* in Chapter 6).

Bystanders can experience anxiety and fear – if they see that no one has intervened, they may worry that they too might get bullied. If the victim is a friend of theirs, they might break off the relationship worried that they might soon become embroiled in the bully's actions or that they will lose status from being seen socialising with the victim. They may even blame their friend for inviting the negative attention.

Bystanders can also feel guilty and helpless for not standing up to the bully or for getting help. Some might be persuaded to join in with the bullying over time: children who observe violent behaviour without negative consequences for the bully are more likely to use aggression in the future.

General advice for parents to stop bullying behaviour

Ask your child about her day and her friendships to find out if she is being treated negatively – or treating other children negatively. If you recognise any bullying behaviour directed at, or by, your child, talk it through and suggest ways for your child to deal with it – as victim or bully. If your child insists there is nothing wrong but you are still concerned by her behaviour, contact the school to say that you are worried and explain why. Someone should follow it up.

Check your understanding of what your child wants to say and how he feels: 'So you think your teacher's picking on you? . . . I can see this has upset you . . . '

Avoid having attitudes such as, 'Being bullied never did me any harm,' and, 'Bullying is part of growing up – it builds character,' and, 'Boys will be boys,' and, 'Sticks and stones may break my bones but words will never hurt me.' They are not useful in stopping bullying behaviour or in helping a child who is being bullied.

Avoid showing prejudices. For example, if your child hears you speak derogatively of other races or of homosexuality, that message will be replayed in school. Instead show tolerance and show an expectation that your child is tolerant of other people, of their beliefs and of their lifestyles. You also need to allow for the fact that your child might grow up to be lesbian or gay, for example. Let your child know that you will love her just as much whatever her sexuality.

Tell your child that he should refuse to join in any bullying and report any bullying that he sees. He should also try to diffuse any rising conflict by ignoring what was said or by walking away. But he should tell you about what happened so that you can discuss future tactics.

Be a strong role model for prosocial behaviour. Apologise to your child when you make a mistake – and ask for an apology when she does something hurtful to you. Allow your child to correct you; this should make her more receptive to you when you tell her off.

Show care to friends and neighbours. For example, when a neighbour has a crisis such as bereavement, help out with preparing food, shopping or looking after her children. Let your child hear you express your sympathy and discuss with him how sad it is for your neighbour. It is especially important for boys to see their fathers in a caring role.

When you see someone in trouble, ask to help. I was in an out-of-town shopping centre, returning to my car. An elderly couple passed my daughter and me, walking towards the shops. The man had to stop every few paces to cling onto a bollard to get his breath back. I asked if they wanted help and for me to get a wheelchair for him. This is not to suggest that children should offer to help strangers but to follow your example by offering to help a child in distress in school.

It is also important for your child to see you intervene to help other people or to put something right. Adrian was travelling on the train when a group of rugby supporters got on. They lit up. Adrian pointed to the No Smoking sign and said, 'Smoking in trains is not allowed.' Although the supporters did not put out their cigarettes straight away, other passengers became emboldened and backed Adrian up. The supporters extinguished their cigarettes. Again, it would be inappropriate for a child to challenge a train full of adults. However, witnessing the effect of one person saying something and having all the bystanders join in might encourage your child to speak out when he witnesses bullying behaviour in school.

Also be careful not to drop litter and to check that your child doesn't drop it – this shows respect for other people and the local community. Be friendly to your local shopkeepers and impress upon your child to be polite to them, especially if you use a corner shop – show you value the convenience of having them open early until late, sympathise with the long hours they must keep and ask after their health.

Encourage your child to talk about feelings by sharing how you feel about something that's happened or how you feel about your day. This will make it more natural for your child to confide in you when something has gone wrong alerting you to bullying issues early. Talking about what has happened will help her feel supported. This can give her emotional strength to deal with the bullying and seek help from you, friends and teachers if necessary. Boys can find it especially hard to reveal how they feel, so living with a father who does admit to vulnerabilities and talks about emotional issues can help boys become more open.

Have clear boundaries and consequences as a framework to living as a family but do be prepared to negotiate and listen to your child. This makes her feel respected and will give her high self-esteem; qualities that are needed in challenging bullying behaviour.

When you know that your child is being bullied

Tell your child how she could protect herself. She should avoid the bullies whenever possible, avoid going places where they are known to 'hang out' and avoid lonely places where she might be trapped by them. She could also vary any routes she takes so that her movements are not predictable and ask her friends to stay with her for protection.

Tell your child not to give bullies the satisfaction of seeing that what they do upsets him – it will increase their gratification. However, it can be useful for the bullies to know how their behaviour has affected your child once an adult has helped increase their empathy for him.

Tell your child not to retaliate as this can make the bullying escalate and can get her into trouble – and the bullies might be seen by teachers as the injured ones. This also includes not replying to cyber bullying messages – and your child shouldn't send a message when she is angry as that can invite retaliation.

Suggest ways for your child to distract bullies by making a joke or getting them to divert their attention elsewhere. Your child could try asking the bullies to repeat what they have just said, if it is verbal bullying, to try to make them feel small and make them a point of fun in the view of bystanders.

Ask your child to act confidently even if he doesn't feel confident.

Tell your child not to blame herself for being bullied – it is not her fault. For support, she could call ChildLine.

Ask your child to make a diary of every bullying incident

and note who witnessed these events to make teachers take his claims seriously.

Ask your child to save evidence of bullying such as text and email messages. If there's a website, online voting site, weblog, or message board that says bad things about your child, she should save a copy or print it out.

Help your child report cyber bullying to his mobile phone company, his Internet Service Provider, the host of an offensive website, the chatroom moderator and the police – it's against the law to make a call or send a text or email message that's abusive or threatening, or to keep sending messages that annoy or scare people. If he is being bullied by someone from his school, he should let the school know. If a school email address is being used, the school will be able to find out who is using it.

Help prevent your child from being cyber bullied again. She should change her chatroom ID details so that the bully won't recognise her again and she must not put her photo in her chatroom profile. It helps to use an anonymous sounding email address too if someone wants to contact her out of the chatroom – but she should always be very careful about doing this as the person might not be safe. She should also block bullies' email addresses and be selective about who she adds to her contacts list in the future.

If your child is being bullied through a mobile phone, she could change her number and be careful who she gives her new number to. Alternatively, she can block the bully's number but the bully might borrow someone else's phone to bother her.

If your child gets a new number – and some mobile phone companies will let children change for free if they are being bullied – she should tell all her friends to keep the number secret and not to leave their phones where other children can pick them up to scroll through their address book. She should not record her own phone message on her mobile phone or give her name on answering so that the bullies won't know if they have the right number. Neither should she answer calls on her mobile when the caller's number is not recognised by an entry in her phone address book.

Don't go directly to the parents of the bullying children – should you know who they are – as they might not be sympathetic and they could deny that their child is at fault which would make matters worse. Using the school to intervene on your behalf will make them take the matter more seriously and may bring to light other complaints about the same child.

Contact your child's school with a full written report to ensure they have all the facts, that you have evidence of having given them the details and that they will take the matter seriously.

Avoid unhelpful behaviour when dealing with your child's school such as becoming very angry, demanding that the bullies be harshly punished. Wait to listen to what the school proposes to do first and then question staff over the appropriateness of the approach using what you know of bullying to help you.

Ask the school what they are going to do to make sure your child is safe. Will the bullies' parents be told about what has happened? Talk to friends who have children at the same school and ask if their children can help support your child, especially if he is bullied on the way to or from school.

Contact a parent support line such as Parentline Plus. They will help you deal with any difficult behaviour your child has because of the bullying and will advise you on how to deal with what's happened.

Don't get angry with your child for being bullied – but also be prepared to hear more than your child's version of what went on. If your child is partly to blame, you need to discuss this with her and discuss with the school what you should do about it. Tell your child that you are there to help her regardless of what happened and that you hope she will let you give her the support she needs.

Don't show disappointment that a boy 'can't stand up for himself and be a man' as that will destroy his self-esteem. Also, don't insist he joins a self-defence class as many children do not feel comfortable with this, or they might have a disability that prevents them from learning these skills – it should only be suggested as an option.

Don't suggest ways in which your child could punish the bullies as it could escalate the bullying and introduce weapons.

Involve the police if your child has been physically attacked or seriously threatened.

Withdraw your child from school temporarily if you don't feel the school is effectively addressing the bullying and you worry for your child's physical or emotional safety – but you do need a doctor's certificate to authorise his absence so that you are not prosecuted for failing to ensure your child's attendance at school. Or you could withdraw him permanently and offer home education, supported by an organisation such as Education Otherwise. Badly affected children should be given counselling.

When you know that your child is bullying

Consider your contribution to your child's behaviour. It has been found that children are more likely to bully if they come from homes where there is little emotional support, attention or warmth; where parents don't appear to worry where their children are or how late they stay out or whether they do their school work; and who model aggressive – verbal or physical – behaviour at home. When children are treated with violence they can treat other children with violence; some children who bully are also victims of bullying at home. Very lax or over-strict parenting also increase the risk of bullying.

Avoid unhelpful attitudes when dealing with your child's school such as saying, 'My child would never do something like that!'; 'That's not bullying, it's just playing around'; 'This kind of thing helps toughen kids up,' and, 'You're blowing this out of all proportion.'

Don't accept that the bullying was only done in fun and that the other child didn't mind (see *Is it really just fun?* in Chapter 8).

Take it seriously if your child has been bullying – not just for the sake of the victim but also for the sake of your child. If you don't do anything about it, your child will get the message that her behaviour is acceptable and she will be more likely to have other antisocial behaviour. However, don't physically punish your child as that will increase her aggression, especially towards her victim.

Change home rules to keep a close eye on what your child is doing and spend more time with him. Deny privileges until they are earned back by positive behaviour and use non-violent sanctions appropriate to the level of severity of the misdemeanour and your child's age.

Teach prosocial behaviour by example. If you want your child to stop swearing, or to stop talking to you disrespectfully, you must make sure you don't swear at her or talk to her disrespectfully. Don't gossip unkindly about people or make fun of them – it will encourage your child to do the same. Show how to be a good friend by being a good friend to your friends. Show your child that a more effective way of achieving social dominance is through co-operative and positive social behaviour rather than through aggressive means.

Be consistent in your expectations of your child following home rules.

Praise your child when he does something positive or honours a rule he previously used to break.

Always be calm when you deal with your child and refrain from being hostile or aggressive – or that will encourage her to behave in the same way with other children.

Question your child about the friends he sees and the values they have – are they encouraging him to behave aggressively? Are they likely to encourage him into more trouble such as criminal behaviour?

Keep in touch with your child's school to monitor her behaviour. When there has been an improvement in school behaviour and school work, praise your child and gradually return privileges – with the warning that they can be withdrawn again at any time.

When your child witnesses bullying

Be sure to be interested in your child's day even when she isn't talking about something that happened to her. It is important you are familiar with the culture of the school, and anecdotes help give you a fuller picture. Many parents complain that their children don't tell them anything about the school day – so be grateful if your child does and reward her by showing that you are following what she is saying: 'Really?' and by asking questions: 'So when did that happen?'

Be concerned for children of other parents in the same way you hope that they would show concern if they were hearing about something bad happening to your child. Although something has not happened to your child now, it doesn't mean that he won't find himself in a similar situation later.

Go over the essential details to check your understanding once your interest is sparked in a bullying incident related to you by your child. When did this happen? Who did what to whom? How did it start? How long has this kind of thing been going on? Who saw it? Did any teachers see it or get told about it? If so, what did they do?

Although your child may not know all the answers to your questions, you will at least have some facts verified and get a rough background picture.

Ask your child how she felt about seeing the bullying. What did her friends think? Did they wonder whether they should do anything about it? This may come as a surprise – most children are happy to stay in the background and be anonymous witnesses. But intervene?

Comfort your child if she has been upset by anything she witnessed. Encourage her to talk about how she felt at the time and how she feels now.

Ask your child how he would feel if he were picked on. What would he want friends and other witnesses to do? What could he do now?

Talk about what your child could do about reporting the bullying. Could he talk to a teacher about the incident, talk to his friends and get them as a group to talk to a teacher about it?

If your child doesn't feel comfortable about dealing with it personally, ask his permission for you to ring the school about what he told you. Teachers should take any concerns about your child remaining anonymous seriously so that he doesn't get targeted for having told. However, it gives more power to your child if he can tell directly, albeit in secret – taking control of the situation may make him feel capable of dealing with any bullying that may happen to him.

Discuss how your child can help the victim. For example, she could go up to the victim the next day and ask how she is and sympathise with her. She could say she feels guilty about not doing anything to help – is there anything she could do now? She could, for example, go with the child to tell a teacher or stay with her as protection against a future attack.

Follow up with your child any cases of bullying that he's told you about. Although he may not know the full outcome, especially if the victim isn't in his class, you might find out whether the school has acted positively on information you gave.

When you know the parents of the victim discuss with your child the need for you to phone the parents to tell them what happened in case their child has not told about it. Say that if their child told her parents about your child being bullied, you would definitely want to know and would feel very hurt if they didn't care enough to tell you.

When you ring the parents of the bullied child, ask for the phone call to be kept secret from their child if you think their child will blame your child for telling. Their child might be afraid of reprisals from the bully and so be angry with your child for having told.

Show that you care and ask for an update of what happens with their child – and how the situation gets resolved. This can be useful in case you ever find yourself in a similar situation with your child.

6

CHILDREN WITH SPECIAL EDUCATIONAL NEEDS

In a study by Whitney and others (1994) it was found that children with special educational needs (SEN) are two to three times more likely to be bullied than their peers and are more likely to be bullies themselves. The National Austistic Society (2006) found that over 40 per cent of children with autism and 60 per cent of children with Asperger's Syndrome (essentially high functioning autism) had been bullied at school – by staff as well as by pupils.

Children with SEN may have a medical condition that affects the way they behave, including irritating behaviour and social skills deficits. Since children with SEN are often considered by their peers to have low status, it is common for them to have few or no friends: peer rejection contributes to victimisation.

An understanding of SEN is required to judge whether children have behaved in certain ways, reacted to provocation in certain ways or invited bullying because of a particular difficulty they have. This difficulty may be due to either a diagnosed or an undiagnosed medical condition. Before making quick judgments as to which child in a scrap is at fault, it is important to have all the facts and then examine them in relation to what is known about your child's medical condition – or suggest a referral if a diagnosis of SEN is suspected from your child's behaviour.

Autistic spectrum disorders

Autism is a developmental disability involving a defect in the functioning of the brain and is four times as common in boys as in girls. There is tremendous variation in children with autism which is why the condition has a 'spectrum'; many children with autism are talented and gifted. Although autistic spectrum disorders (ASD) are usually diagnosed in childhood, many children are not diagnosed until their teens or even adulthood.

Children with ASD have difficulties in three areas: social interaction, communication and behaviour and each can present problems in relation to being bullied.

Problems with social interaction

Not understanding body language. Children with ASD can misinterpret another child's threatening behaviour as an effort to be friendly and find it hard to display appropriate body language themselves, having a limited use of gestures and facial expressions. They find it hard to make eye contact and can have a fixed gaze.

Failing to develop peer relationships at an appropriate level for their development – they do not understand social expectations such as allowing another child equal time to speak, not interrupting and not making irrelevant comments, and they have trouble seeing things from another child's perspective or understanding how he might feel.

Being anxious about social situations. Children with ASD like structure and routine but social situations, especially with other children, are unpredictable and easy to get wrong particularly as children with ASD don't understand them. Jokes and sarcasm are particularly hard for children with ASD to grasp.

Having low self-esteem. Children with ASD may take literally all the negative things people say about them – either casually or in bullying situations – and ascribe them as lifelong failings. Children with ASD are also found to be frequently in the wrong – but they often don't understand why. Low self-esteem can prevent children with ASD from standing up to bullies or from seeking help when bullied.

Finding it hard, or impossible, to lie. Children with ASD believe that everyone else knows what they are thinking – they don't understand that other people have different feelings and thoughts from them – so they may get their friends into trouble and be seen as 'snitches'. It also means that very young children with ASD cannot play games such as *Hide and Seek* and older children with ASD will not understand about being tactful.

Being accused of bullying despite the lack of intent most bullies have. For example, a child with ASD might want to make friends with someone who doesn't want to become friends, pulling the other child towards him; or he might insist on joining in a game with other children who don't want him to.

Being unable to predict what might happen next. Children with ASD can be naïve so cannot flag up behaviour as trouble-some.

Unquestioningly carrying out something a bully has asked them to. Children with ASD can get into trouble or put themselves in danger – and they might easily imitate bullying behaviour carried out on them with other children without realising they are doing wrong.

Problems with communication

Having delayed speech or lack of development of speech. When they have learned to talk, some children with ASD talk too little and some talk too much, dominating conversations.

Lacking variation in rhythm, volume, pitch and melody of speech. Children with ASD can also fail to pick up changes in meaning from other people's use of stressing particular words in a sentence.

Being unable to initiate or sustain a conversation. Children with ASD also fail to understand that conversation is meant to be two-way rather than talking at the other person.

Taking what is said literally. For example, a teacher saying, 'You need to try harder. It's time you pulled your socks up,' may well result in a child with ASD confusedly trying to tug on socks that are already pulled up while wondering what the connection is with his work. The child won't understand why the others in the class laugh which adds to his confusion.

Problems with behaviour

Restricted and repetitive behaviour. Children with ASD may have an interest in something that is abnormal in intensity or focus and can have a persistent preoccupation with parts of objects which can irritate or bore other children. (A sudden change in their special interest from a benign subject to weaponry and violence may suggest they are being bullied.)

Having an inflexible need to keep to routines and rituals. Children with ASD can become very distressed if something disrupts a routine – such as an unexpected change to the school day, or ritual – such as always sitting in the same chair, wearing the same clothes, eating the same for lunch or avoiding a particular colour.

Having repetitive mannerisms such as hand flapping or complex body movements.

In puberty there can be a temporary increase in the way the condition is expressed which makes children with ASD more prone to being bullied.

Common conditions that coexist with ASD

Many children with ASD commonly have other disorders as well. These include Attention Deficit Hyperactivity Disorder (see page 68), anxieties and phobias, sensitivities to smell, sound, light, touch and taste, and Developmental Coordination Disorder (formerly called dyspraxia).

Developmental Coordination Disorder is an impairment of the organisation of movement affecting the planning of what to do and how to do it. Children who have Developmental Coordination Disorder have difficulties with motor skills such as getting dressed, tying shoe laces, kicking and catching balls, and dancing and so are more likely to do passive activities in their spare time like reading and watching television. Not spending much free time with other children delays the development of their social skills and so they are more likely to handle relationships ineptly.

Children with Developmental Coordination Disorder are often bullied – because they are clumsy and because they have few friends – which can make them aggressive, hostile and anxious. During puberty, with increased self-consciousness, they may be more sensitive to negative comments from other children.

How schools can protect children with ASD from being bullied

Have a safe place for children to go to during break times and lunchtimes, when children with ASD are most vulnerable – they often seek solitude which makes them easy targets. Ask if your child can spend break times in the school's special unit or library – or in a designated classroom. Because children with ASD can get anxious when there is no routine, or their time is not structured, it is also helpful for them to be given something to do while being supervised.

Have a 'friendship bench' in primary school for children to sit on if they need someone to talk to or to play with.

Train older children as schoolyard 'angels' to support younger children in primary school; they can be identified by a badge. When schoolyard 'angels' see children sitting alone on the friendship bench they go to them to keep them company or to help them join in with other children's games.

Train adult volunteers to organise games or activities at break times and in how to encourage children to join in.

Set up a buddying system – other children take children with ASD under their wing, explaining things like: rules of schoolyard games, jokes, why they must ask permission to join in other children's games, why they can't push in when queuing. In secondary school, buddies could help more discreetly to check that a child is safe and happy to avoid drawing unwelcome attention to their role.

Buddies do need some training on what to do if the children they are buddying are being bullied – so that they don't deal aggressively with the situation and don't take advantage of their responsibility.

Set up a 'circle of friends' – a small group of volunteer children is informed about ASD and helps teach other children about the condition: the group also teaches children with ASD social skills and schoolyard rules and expectations, helping to prevent them from being bullied and raising their self-esteem through social acceptance. For detailed information, contact Autism Helpline, part of The National Autistic Society. This approach can be used to help children with other SEN too – and it may reduce the bullying of siblings without ASD who are targeted because a brother or sister has the condition.

Use circle time in primary schools to talk about bullying and to help children understand the way other children feel about things. During circle time, whatever children say is respected – no one is allowed to make fun of them or laugh at them. And because the children sit in a circle, there is no hierarchy – they are all equal and their contributions are equally valued. Circle time also encourages eye contact between speakers and listeners which helps increase children's feeling of connectedness to their peers and helps them gain interpersonal skills.

Display a feelings chart – to help children who cannot verbalise how they are feeling raise concerns by pointing to a face depicting the emotion they are experiencing. Because children with ASD may not know what bullying behaviour is, they won't be able to tell their teacher what has happened but by pointing to an unhappy or scared face, teachers can try to find out why children are feeling like this. However, children with ASD will need first to be taught what these expressions mean.

Teach social skills to help prevent children with ASD invite bullying through clumsy social interactions, attention seeking and provocative behaviour. This will also help reduce the shyness some children with ASD have and help them make friends so that they are more popular and less solitary. However, children with ASD will have to be taught what to do for every social situation that comes up: they cannot adapt information to different circumstances.

Teaching social skills can also help children with ASD identify bullying behaviour. However, this may not help when bullies falsely befriend them. It may also be hard for children with ASD to distinguish between friendly and malign teasing: some children with ASD develop paranoia once they have understood they have been bullied, thinking everyone is out to bully them.

Teach anger management – to help children with ASD deal with frustration and aggression.

Teach assertiveness skills – show how children with ASD can respond to bullying in non-violent and non-confrontational ways.

Have a 'suggestion box' – verbal communication can be hard for children with ASD so writing down what has happened gives them more time to think about what they want to say and how they want to say it. Calling the box a 'bullying box' is not helpful since it can alert other children about a child who has 'told'.

Attention Deficit Hyperactivity Disorder

Attention Deficit Hyperactivity Disorder (ADHD) is a hereditary behavioural disorder that affects mostly boys: about three times as many boys have been diagnosed with ADHD than girls although it has been argued that more girls may actually have the condition but be undiagnosed because they tend not to be as disruptive in school as boys with the condition.

Jadad and others (1999) found that about 70 per cent of children with ADHD will continue to have some difficulties in adolescence and 65 per cent in adulthood – impulsivity and restlessness may have declined but inattention, problems with short-term memory and frustration with learning may remain.

Many children with ADHD who have been prescribed medication to manage their symptoms feel uncomfortable about taking their medication in school; some have said they have been picked on because of it. However, longer acting stimulant preparations are now available which can be taken once daily at breakfast time. This is particularly helpful to children who were avoiding their lunchtime dose in school for fear of stigmatisation.

Symptoms of ADHD in children

Having poor social skills – and a poor understanding of social expectations. Children with ADHD often interrupt conversations, call out in class and find it hard to wait their turn. They may also misread facial expressions and not understand teasing, immediately reacting to any slight they think they might have been given.

Having low self-esteem. Children with ADHD often fail in school, which gives them low self-esteem. And because other children and adults often don't understand their condition, frequently getting angry with them or being rude to them, it further diminishes their self-esteem. This can increase their frustration – and aggression.

Acting impulsively. Children with ADHD often act without considering the consequences of their actions. This can make it more likely that they take part in dangerous activities – and their actions may lead to expulsion. It also makes them accident prone.

Being insatiable – being demanding or interrogative without knowing when to stop.

Being inattentive – although the level of distraction in children with ADHD can vary throughout the day or from day to day, as can their mood swings. Their poor short-term memory can affect turning up to school with the right books and equipment as well as their learning. Although children with ADHD are not lacking in intelligence they do have trouble in getting work done.

Over-reacting to an event escalates the conflict and can often result in fights – for which children with ADHD can be blamed – and since they give such a big response to teasing they are prime targets for bullying.

Having antisocial or delinquent behaviour.

Being restless, having poor coordination and being highly disorganised are also traits in children with ADHD.

In puberty, social interactions may become more difficult

as the bossiness and blurting out of inappropriate comments children with ADHD may make can result in them feeling more insecure and self-conscious than before. It can also make teachers punish them for insolence.

Common conditions that coexist with ADHD

The conditions mentioned below are not part of ADHD itself but are often present in children with ADHD.

Conduct disorder is a behavioural disorder characterised by a repetitive and persistent pattern of antisocial, aggressive or defiant behaviour such as fighting or bullying, cruelty to others or to animals, severe destructiveness to property, stealing, setting fire to things, repeated lying and truancy from school. Children with conduct disorder can also have severe temper tantrums and defiant provocative behaviour. Conduct disorder is frequently associated with unsatisfactory family relationships and failure at school – and is more common in boys.

Oppositional defiant disorder (ODD) is another behavioural disorder characterised by markedly defiant, disobedient provocative behaviour but with the absence of more severe antisocial and aggressive acts. Children with ODD are also rude, unco-operative and resist authority, actively defying adults or rules; they deliberately annoy other people, are confrontational and tend to be angry, resentful and easily lose their temper. They frequently blame other people for their mistakes or difficulties, are not remorseful and are openly hostile.

Although more commonly found in boys in very young children, the incidence of ODD in girls increases as they get older, evening out the differences. Children with ODD commonly bully – they are impulsive and aggressive.

Ian Wallace, an Australian ADHD and ODD specialist, advises avoiding face-to-face confrontations and battles with children with ODD; instead reduce your child's hostility by not staring at him – look away – and use off-hand cool responses. Suggest alternatives and let your child choose which one to take – trying to enforce your authority will immediately increase hostility. And avoid arguing!

Specific learning difficulties such as dyslexia often coexist with ADHD and children may need one-to-one help or the use of a computer instead of having to write, and they may need more time in exams.

Tourette's Syndrome is having sudden and repeated body movements known as motor tics – such as eye blinking, or jumping; or vocalisations, known as vocal tics – such as throat clearing, barking or shouting out obscenities. None of these is controllable. About 50 per cent of people with Tourette's Syndrome have ADHD (but not vice versa).

Other common conditions that occur with ADHD include ASD, depression and anxiety.

How schools can help children with ADHD escape being bullied – and from bullying

As for children with ASD, it is important to teach social skills and assertiveness skills to children with ADHD – and for teachers to explain to the class why pupils should not provoke children with ADHD. Teaching anger management can also be of help.

Ian Wallace says it is important not to escalate a problem involving children with ADHD. Quick intervention is needed using a firm, monotonous voice in brief sentences. Harsh discipline and criticism are to be avoided as are long debates and reasoning. Children with ADHD are often suspended for aggressive behaviour after having been goaded by other children. Getting angry with a child with ADHD just inflames the child – instead the child needs to be soothed.

7

RAISING CHILDREN'S
SELF-ESTEEM

Although being bullied can make children have low self-esteem, it is often low self-esteem that makes children vulnerable to victimisation in the first place. And having low self-esteem makes it more likely that children blame themselves for being bullied – and less likely that they will seek help to stop it. They may think that if they weren't so short or fat or stupid, they would not have invited teasing and worse.

Part of having high self-esteem is children knowing that it is OK to be different – and that they are OK. It is also OK to make mistakes – everyone does; they shouldn't be so hard on themselves. Children also need to be kind to themselves, forgive themselves and regularly treat themselves – they are worth it!

Raising victims' self-esteem gives victims the confidence to challenge bullies and the self-respect they need to get help in making an adult listen as soon as something hurtful is done. However, children who maintain their self-esteem through bullying – gaining pride from dominating other children – can also benefit from having their self-esteem boosted in more positive ways, which may diminish their desire to bully.

How teachers can raise children's self-esteem
Children should be shown warmth – children can tell if teachers don't like them. Polly, when in primary school, said

her class teacher didn't like her. When asked, 'How can you tell? What makes you think that?' she replied, 'Because she smiles and says hello to my friends but she ignores me.' To have to spend an entire school year believing that their teacher does not like them – and having strong evidence for it – will damage children's self-esteem.

Children should be praised whenever possible so that they are taught in a positive and rewarding environment. It also gives pupils an incentive to do more of what got them praise in the first place – and get even more praise.

Teachers should group children into teams for PE lessons involving games if it obvious that some will be rejected. This prevents a child always being the last, or nearly last, to be picked. Another reason for teachers to pair off children or form them into groups is to achieve well balanced teams with a good mix of abilities within each.

Children who need extra help should be seated with children who can give it. For example, children with social skills deficits could be seated with socially confident children to give them more opportunity to pick up communication skills. Seating trouble makers next to children who work hard discourages the trouble makers from deviant behaviour and makes them more likely to settle down and achieve something during the lesson.

Teachers should be sensitive to what children find hard. They shouldn't force a child to answer a question in front of the class if he looks scared about it – he will just feel humiliated when he gets it wrong. If a child does not want to take his turn at reading out loud to the class and the teacher knows from past experience that his stammering has resulted in sniggering, she should pass on to the next child. The teacher could either listen to the child read in private or make a note in his homework diary for someone at home to listen to him read so that eventually he won't feel so scared about reading in class.

Instructions given should be clear – and understanding should be regularly checked – so that children are most likely to succeed. Teachers should invite children to ask questions if they don't understand without fear of being made to feel small about it or they should repeat instructions to the whole class if they suspect some children have misunderstood.

Something I found helpful after explaining a difficult concept in physics was asking children to put up their hands if they thought they understood what I had said. I told them that I only expected about half the class to understand at that stage. Half of the class did put up their hands. Had I asked children to identify themselves as not having understood by raising their hands I might not have had a single hand raised.

Expectations should be clear so that children don't unexpectedly get into trouble or feel that teachers have changed rules just to pick on them. Children should be praised and rewarded for staying within teachers' expectations. For example, teachers could say, 'As you have all worked very hard today we'll pack up now so that you can leave as soon as the bell goes. But no rushing out – wait for me to tell you which row can go first.' They can reward individuals too – by allowing that child to leave first. A pupil who has misbehaved could, for example, be asked to leave last – giving incentive to behave the next lesson.

Teachers should also be clear on how they expect children to relate to them and with other pupils: 'When someone talks to you, it is polite to stop what you are doing, look the person in the face and listen to what he has to say. When he has finished speaking, you can reply. It's rude to interrupt.'

Responsibilities should be shared out – teachers shouldn't always ask the same children to hand out textbooks, for example. But in case some children use the opportunity to take liberties it should be explained that there is to be no throwing of the books – they have to be either handed to children or placed on the desk in front of them.

Teachers should demand respect for themselves and for all the children present. They should never deliberately embarrass a child, make a joke at her expense, or pick on a child. They should point out any disrespectful behaviour between the children – and ask for apologies to be given. If a child does not know how to make amends, a suggestion could be offered:

'Ben, it was not helpful to thump Joshua because he threw the pen you asked to borrow at you. Instead, say that it was dangerous to throw the pen and you would like him to apologise. Joshua, when Ben asks for an apology I expect you to say sorry.'

Particular difficulties a child has should be explained to the others in the class so that they become more understanding and tolerant. However, in secondary school, children might be too self-conscious to feel comfortable about everyone knowing their difficulties but may appreciate a close friend, or the person they mainly sit with in class, being told.

Teachers should openly value children with disabilities to raise the social status of those children in the class which can help protect them against victimisation.

Teachers should give attention to quiet children as well as to noisy ones. In trying to deal with behaviour problems in class, quiet children are often all but ignored which lowers their self-esteem, and noisy children are rewarded for negative behaviour – they may feel getting negative attention is better than no attention at all. Teachers should try to reward the quiet children for getting on with their work in a co-operative manner and try to focus attention on the positive things the noisy children do rather than noticing them for negative behaviour.

Teachers should separate children in class who demonstrate antisocial behaviour so that they cannot use the lesson to reinforce negative behaviour through group approval.

How parents can raise children's self-esteem

Tell your child that you love him – and that you always will. Showing love and care with physical affection as well as through what you say and do for him also balance out the negative impressions he has of himself through the boundaries that you set and enforce.

Praise your child. Show you value her. Congratulate her on any achievement, however small. Celebrate big achievements. Sometimes give rewards such as staying up a little later, being taken bowling or to the cinema.

Say, and show, how proud you are of your child. To augment your praise, tell interested family and friends of his achievements. Remind him of his strengths and the things you like about him.

Commiserate with your child for any disappointment she might experience – say that not doing well bears no relation to how she is valued as a person. Remind her that failures are only failures if they aren't used as learning experiences.

Avoid as much criticism as you can and, when you do have to criticise, try to make it constructive so that your child knows for the next time: 'If you only fill the mug half full it won't spill so easily when you carry it . . .'

Ask your child's opinion on things – to show that his opinions and thoughts are important to you. Sometimes ask advice – it will encourage him to come to you for advice as well as showing him that you feel he has something of value to contribute.

Apologise if you have done something wrong or something that's hurt your child's feelings. Treat her with the same respect that you'd like her to show you. She will be more forgiving when someone makes a mistake with her and making the effort to apologise shows her that she has worth.

Be prepared to change your mind if you realise you made the wrong decision against your child and explain your change of heart. But don't give in to whining and other typical child pressure!

Don't have over high expectations – your child will feel pressurised and will worry you won't love him if he does not get, for example, the grades you hoped for. But don't have such low expectations that your child believes you think him useless or not capable of much – that, too, can lower his self-esteem.

Remind your child that she has rights (see below) and needs like everyone else. She needs to work at upholding her rights with other people, including her friends, and to let people know her needs.

Reassure your child that as long as his life is moving forward in some way, he's doing fine. He does not have to measure himself against others to feel good. He should only be compared with how he was and how he is now.

Occasionally give your child treats of some kind, just for being her. They don't always have to come as a reward for doing something right or for succeeding in something. If they were, your child would get the message that she doesn't deserve treats unless she has done something noteworthy.

Don't overreact to bad behaviour – but don't excuse it either. Explain how your child should have behaved and what you expect in the future. Say how disappointed you are. Instead of physical punishment, use other strategies such as not watching television or playing computer games, losing pocket money, going to bed early and 'grounding'.

Don't talk negatively about your child in his hearing. It will lower his self-esteem and make him angry with you.

Don't put your child down by saying things like, 'I might have known you wouldn't manage to pour that without spilling it everywhere.' Put-downs also tend to label a person – it is your child's behaviour you need to address, not your child. What you could say instead is, 'That wasn't very successful. You need to practise more and then you'll be able to do it without spilling it.'

Don't blame your child for something that was not her fault – listen to get all the facts before you cast judgment. Also avoid blaming by saying, 'Look what you made me do!' You cannot blame a child for your inattention. If you know you need to concentrate on something say, 'Just wait a moment while I do this – I don't want to drop it.' Otherwise she will feel very hurt and resentful.

Make the majority of your interactions with your child positive so that there is not undue conflict in the house – however, this can be extremely hard when children are in the throes of puberty. When there is high conflict, try to damp it down by not rising to irritations and by acting calmly.

Enjoy your child – try to have some fun every day. Share jokes and watch television together and talk about what you see. Show that you value his company.

If your child seems upset ask her about it, don't ignore it.

Trust your child and give him age appropriate responsibility so that he has a chance to develop. If trust is broken say how hurt you feel to show him the consequences of breaking trust.

Recognise your child's sensitivity

Although it is always wrong to stop immediately what you are doing to give your child undivided attention – after all, she does need to know she is not the only person who has things to do and needs to fulfil – your child does deserve some attention all to herself. For example, when she is proud of a painting she did at school and comes in running, holding it out in front of her, saying, 'Mummy, look what I've done today!', it would be unkind to say, 'Not now darling. I'm busy.'

While writing this book, I received a magazine with a cheque through the post. When my 15-year-old daughter came in, I said excitedly, 'Look, I've had an article published in this magazine.' She said, 'I'll come and see in a minute. I've just got to get my drink from my bedroom.' I felt quite deflated. Didn't she realise that this couldn't wait? Wasn't she just as excited as me? Well, no. Obviously not.

The words she used were the same words I have used with her many a time. 'Yes, but let me do this first . . .' and, 'In a moment. This won't take long . . .' and, 'I've just got to . . . and then I'll be with you.'

If I, as an adult, felt let down by my daughter's temporary rejection, how much more must a child feel it? By the time my daughter did come to look, my excitement had diminished. She said, 'Lovely. Well done,' as though our roles were reversed and she was the mother and I the child.

Even if half of the time we, as parents, can listen when we are asked, it will do much to raise our children's self-esteem and show how important we think they are. When they don't have to fight for our attention and make a second or even third attempt at telling us when something went wrong at school, or on the way home, they will know that we care and that telling is the right thing to do.

Recognise personal rights

Everyone has personal rights but few people are aware of them. These rights apply to your child as well as to you. By knowing these rights and not violating them, you show your child respect – and when your child becomes familiar with them, he is more likely to demand respect from you and from children at school.

1. I have the right to state my needs.
2. I have the right to be respected and treated as an equal.
3. I have the right to some time alone and for privacy.
4. I have the right to make my own decisions and take responsibility for them.
5. I have the right to say 'yes' and 'no' to others and have my decision accepted.
6. I have the right to change my mind.
7. I have the right to ask for things to be explained without being made fun of.
8. I have the right to be myself without people trying to change me.
9. I have the right to be successful.
10. I have the right to change any part of me.

Although point 8 states, 'I have the right to be myself without people trying to change me', this does not mean that children have a right to bully – as that violates other people's rights to be respected and treated as equals.

By emphasising point 10, 'I have the right to change any part of me', children know that who they are now does not necessarily limit who they may become in the future. We can all improve throughout our lives to become people we are proud to be.

Social skills and self-esteem

If your child's social skills are very poor she is not likely to get positive reactions from other people which will dent her self-esteem. Some children need to have social skills formally taught.

Make a list of things you need to work on with your child and prioritise the skills with the most essential first so that your child can then build on the successes of those. Overwhelming her with a barrage of social rules will only lower her self-esteem as there will be too much to think of at once and so she will flounder. Praise your child however slight her progress. All effort should be praised too.

Body language and self-esteem

Most children are very adept at recognising slight changes in the way people speak to them, telling them what people think of them. If you are to raise your child's self-esteem, the messages he needs to receive are that you like him, you approve of him, you are proud of him for his individual achievements and you enjoy his company. It is also essential that your child is confident of your love. Teachers, too, need to be aware of their body language.

Negative messages are given by: frowning, tightening of your lips, narrowing of your eyes, sneering, sounding disdainful, being sarcastic, having a hard tone to your voice, sounding cold and distant.

Even how far you stand from your child and your posture can suggest you don't like her. The further away you are, the more you dislike her. If you have your arms folded across your chest you are blocking her from warmth and intimacy, perhaps even being threatening or hostile. Standing tall when you talk to your child when she is small and seated is also showing you want to be cold and distant.

Positive messages are given by: smiling, laughing, speaking with a warm and soft voice, crouching down to talk at your child's level.

8

INCREASING CHILDREN'S EMPATHY

Sympathy and empathy are words with similar meanings but there is a subtle difference. When you sympathise with someone you acknowledge what has happened to her, you express a desire to make things better for her and you express sorrow that something has gone wrong for her. When you empathise with someone you 'put yourself in the other person's shoes' – you perceive how she feels, experience how she feels and understand her situation, feelings and motives as though they were your own.

Having high empathy for others increases feelings of care and diminishes feelings of anger, hostility and hatred – emotions which can lead to bullying. Since children who bully progressively lose empathy for their victims, and bystanders do not feel sufficient empathy for the victim to intervene, increasing empathy among children is essential in tackling bullying. Increased awareness of children's sensitivity may also help adults intervene sooner.

Predicting feelings

To help your child develop empathy ask him first to imagine he is the victim in the situations given below. Then discuss the answers to the following questions: How do you think this person feels and thinks about what has happened? What effect do you think the situation might have on the person? Then ask your child to imagine he is a bystander and discuss: What could you say or do to help the person?

Situation 1
Angharad had removable braces fitted. Girls outside her friendship group got paperclips and put them in their mouths saying, 'Oh, what nice braces we have.'

Possible feelings and thoughts: Angharad might feel embarrassed, hurt and ugly to look at. She might think that everyone thinks the same as the girls who made fun of her.

Possible effects: Angharad might stop smiling so that people won't see her braces. She might not want to wear the braces any more – she might take them out as soon as she leaves home or gets to school which will mean that the position of her teeth and jaw won't be corrected.

To help: Tell off the girls who had made fun of Angharad and tell the teacher what they had done. Reassure Angharad that the girls meant nothing by it other than to be nasty. Say how wonderful her teeth will be when she has finished her treatment. Say that there are many children with crooked teeth – soon plenty of children in the school will be also wearing braces.

Situation 2
Charley has no friends. When a teacher shouts at the whole class he cries; and when children ask about his dad he cries. The others in the class laugh at him and call him a freak because of his behaviour and because he has no friends.

Possible feelings and thoughts: Charley might feel worthless, despised, lonely and isolated from everyone. He might also feel afraid – of other people as well as his dad – and might have lost trust in people generally. He might believe that he will never have a friend or be liked and think that his future is hopeless. He might believe he is a freak and that there is nothing he can do to change it.

Possible effects: Charley might become seriously depressed. He might consider suicide.

To help: There might be no one in Charley's life who takes time to listen or to show him care – he obviously has trouble at home and it looks like he is terrified of his father and of any aggression shown by anyone else. Befriend Charley. Comfort him when he's upset. Don't shout at him. Ask someone in the school to check that he is OK at home.

Situation 3

A group of girls attacks Leonie and Corinne in their class by scribbling on their work, calling them names, spreading untrue rumours about them and writing LOSER in mirror writing on a rubber before stamping it on their faces.

Possible feelings and thoughts: Leonie and Corinne might feel afraid of the girls and of their personal safety, worried about getting into trouble because of their work being messed up, hurt for having their work spoiled, humiliated by having LOSER stamped on their faces and embarrassed by having rumours spread about them. They might feel bad about themselves for allowing it to happen and being powerless to stop it. They might think they really are losers.

Possible effects: The girls might want to avoid school, they might get into trouble by their teachers for handing in messy work and they might distrust other children in their year.

To help: Tell the girls to leave Leonie and Corinne alone. Stop the group of girls from spoiling Leonie and Corinne's work and tell teachers what has happened. Tell everyone that the rumours are untrue and tell the girls how unkind they were to spread them in the first place. Stay near to Leonie and Corinne at break and lunch times.

Situation 4

Girls and boys tell Franco how ugly and disgusting he is. They push each other into him and those who touch him scream and say they'll catch rabies from him. Girls tell him that their friends will go out with him but then the friends say, 'Ugh. I wouldn't go out with him even if he was the last boy on Earth.' Boys trip Franco up and girls write love letters to him pretending they are other girls in the class.

Possible feelings and thoughts: Franco might feel hurt, sad, ugly, worthless and deeply unhappy. He might think the things said about him are personally true, believing he will never find someone to love him.

Possible effects: Franco might become depressed and suicidal; he might avoid school. He might have very low self-esteem, feel unlovable and find it impossible to trust other children.

To help: Don't join in. Tell the others how unkind they are being. Tell teachers what is going on. Befriend Franco and show that some people can be kind and trusted.

Situation 5

Katherine was teased mercilessly because friends made out that she was the only one of the group who had not had sexual inter-course. They called her frigid. One night, at a party, they arranged for a boy to be upstairs in one of the bedrooms and told him to expect Katherine. Then they lured her up to the room and when Katherine was in, held on to the door handle so that she could not escape. Through the door they told Katherine to have sex with the boy. She did. Later she found out that she was the only one of the group who had had sex; they'd lied.

Possible feelings and thoughts: Katherine might feel self-disgust and anger: towards herself for believing the girls and for not standing up to them, towards the girls for persuading her to have sex and towards the boy for what he had done. She might also feel humiliated, embarrassed and soiled. She might be scared of her parents finding out – and scared of the risk of pregnancy and infection, especially if no contraception was used. She might think that she will never trust anyone again.

Possible effects: Katherine's friendship with the girls will be broken or irreparably damaged and she might become friendless. She might become promiscuous from feeling so devalued – now it doesn't matter with whom she has sex or why; the whole act has been spoilt for her. She might have the consequences of an unwanted pregnancy and infection and she might need counselling.

To help: Befriend Katherine and, if no condom was used,

take her to a GUM (genito-urinary medicine) clinic to be checked out for a sexually transmitted infection and ensure she takes the 'morning after pill'. Encourage Katherine to talk about how she feels and comfort her. Try to be there for her long term. Suggest Katherine confides in her parents – although she might feel so mortified that she refuses. If she doesn't want to talk to her parents about what happened, she could ring ChildLine for support.

In the next situation, ask your child to think of how both the bully and the victim feel.

Situation 6
Gavin regularly kicks Rob in the schoolyard at lunch time. Today, the kicks are more vicious than usual. Last night, Gavin had seen his father beat his mother again and this time she had to be taken away in an ambulance. The police said she might not pull through. If she were to die, it would be just Gavin and his dad left in the house.

Possible feelings: Rob might feel scared, angry that he cannot protect himself and humiliated by being kicked on the floor like a dog. He might also be in much physical pain and worry that he might be damaged internally.

Gavin might be angry because of his awful home life, angry with his dad for hurting his mum – and angry with himself for not being able to protect her. He might also be very scared of what will happen to him if his mum is not there to try to protect him. Perhaps his dad will kill him too.

Possible effects: Rob might become depressed and suicidal; he might avoid school.

Gavin's aggression towards Rob might escalate and he might maim or kill Rob.

To help: *Help Rob* by telling teachers. If it won't put them in danger, try with other children to physically restrain Gavin when he kicks Rob until help comes. Encourage Rob to protect himself by telling his parents – who might call the police if the school does not. Support Rob by protecting him from future attacks – never leave him alone.

Help Gavin by telling him to stop hurting Rob and say that Rob has done nothing to deserve being kicked – in any case, differences should be sorted out by talking about them. Ask Gavin why he is behaving like that – where has all his anger come from? Tell Gavin he needs outside help and tell someone who is in a position to get that help for Gavin. Tell Gavin that if he doesn't get help he's likely to get into worse trouble in the future.

Draw on your child's own experiences

Ask your child to discuss times when she has been scared or hurt. Encourage her to talk about her feelings and to question friends or class mates about how they have felt. Your child could point out commonalities to increase feelings of connectedness to other people by saying, 'Oh, I've felt like that too,' or, 'That happened to me once . . .' Explain that exploring vulnerabilities does not make children weak – emotional strength and overcoming adversity are qualities to be admired. Tell your child that if a friend becomes upset while talking about a disturbing event, she should try to comfort him.

Try to draw parallels. If your child has a fear of heights ask how he feels when he is on a tall building or a bridge. Explain that other children might feel the same way but in regard to a spider, or in going to school or in facing a bully.

What role does media violence play on children?

Professor Rowell Huesmann, of the University of Michigan in the USA, studied the effect of television violence on children aged 6 to 10 in 1977, following them up 15 years later in 1992. The study revealed that childhood exposure to media violence predicts young adult aggressive behaviour for both males and females. Identification with aggressive TV characters and perceived realism of TV violence also predict later aggression.

Studies have also suggested that television violence encourages viewers to carry out similar acts. In Merseyside in 1993, two ten-year-old boys abducted, tortured and killed two-year-old James Bulger whose death was similar to that of a child in a film on video the boys had access to the week before the murder.

Playing violent computer games and the like have been thought to be more likely to increase a child's aggression than watching films because, with the games, they are actually taking part in a struggle, are interacting with the game and the game might be played repetitively and involve repeated killing. High levels of violent game exposure have been linked to delinquency, fighting at school and violent criminal behaviour – but these children might have had an aggressive personality to begin with. Not all studies confirm that video game violence does increase aggression and antisocial behaviour and some have suggested that prosocial behaviour, such as co-operation and teamwork, can be developed through playing with a friend.

How schools could counteract the media violence children are exposed to

Schools could make violence real. Timo Nuutinen, who worked at a 'polyclinic' in Finland, made up a slide show of victims' injuries from being bullied such as broken teeth, damaged eyes, broken noses, concussion and even irreversible brain damage. He presented photographs and X-rays of real victims to children at almost every comprehensive school in Finland and explained how the injuries had been made.

Björkqvist and Österman (1999) measured 12- to 16-year-old pupils' attitudes to violence before the slide show, four days after the slide show and again five months later. Both short-term and significant long-term positive effects were found. This was explained in two ways. The children gained very clear information about the consequences of real-life violence – something that watching films doesn't give – of a type which could easily happen to themselves. Also, the children were likely to feel increased empathy towards the victims from seeing the victims' photos and X-rays – which is an effective antidote to aggression. Nuutinen has now extended his work and developed films as well. British schools could collaborate to ask local hospitals to provide the material for a similar presentation.

Schools could show films with bullying themes. For example, the 1999 television drama, *Walking on the Moon*, specifically addresses bullying. Confident and intelligent, 13-year-old Daniel's life is destroyed because he helped a friend who was being bullied: the bullies turned their attention – and aggression – on him and adults did not take his complaints seriously.

The Department for Education and Skills teamed with Actionwork Films to produce the anti-bullying film *Making the Difference* made by young people for young people to promote discussion in schools.

Stories or books about children who are bullied could be read and discussed in class to raise empathy in children.

Schools could have bullying monologues in class or in assembly. The children could either describe something that happened to them and how they felt about it or they could make it up drawing on feelings they have experienced on other occasions. For ideas, see *Is it really just fun?* opposite. The children could enlarge on those, or similar, scenarios.

How parents could counteract the media violence children are exposed to

Watch films with your child involving characters who care about one another and who resolve their difficulties through non-violent means. Usually family films concentrate on these qualities. Discuss what happens and express sympathy when something goes wrong for a character. Ask your child how she would feel if she had been that person to increase her feelings of empathy.

Explain how drama works. There has to be conflict in any story, including family stories. Towards the end of a drama either a workable solution is found or something changes to make the characters' lives happier.

Family problems need to be exaggerated in fiction to give impact and to make it vital that viewers or readers stay with the story, needing to know how the difficulties are eventually resolved. Dramas are designed to keep us guessing to the last, often with increasing tension and conflict, to ensure we don't switch off or put the book aside. Just because your child sees high levels of conflict on the television, or reads about them in a book, this does not mean that all families operate like this or that his should.

Be careful about what a young child watches – if your child does crave some more excitement try to find films and programmes with implied violence rather than ones that show all the gore. Should explicit violence really be seen as entertainment? And be careful about a young child watching the news – hearing about abductions and murders would frighten timid children and suggest to aggressive children that this kind of behaviour is common and therefore, possibly, acceptable.

Discuss fictional or real-life violent events, appropriate to your child's age and emotional development, to re-sensitise your child and get him to understand, for example, the devastation a parent or sibling feels when a child is hurt – or murdered – by school bullies.

Nathanson (1999) suggests that parents watching and commenting on films with their children reduces children's identification with the perpetrator of violence, reduces their perception of the violence as real, and reduces the likelihood that they will rehearse the observed violence later.

Watch documentaries with your child, appropriate to your child's age and emotional development, that highlight national and world social injustices or bring to light special difficulties people have. For example, you could watch and discuss programmes on child slavery, human trafficking, poverty, asylum seekers, children with disabilities or with particular medical conditions or people overcoming personal challenges.

Is it really just fun?

As justification for their behaviour, bullies often say they are just having a bit of fun and that the victim knows they were only teasing or having a joke and that he does not mind. So why doesn't the victim laugh with them? Discuss the following situations with your child.

1. Ethan is overweight. Classmates call him Pig and they send him photos of a dead pig by email. He says, 'I've tried to cut down how much I eat at meal times but later I'm so hungry I raid the cupboards and eat all the kinds of things I should be avoiding. I'll never lose weight and they'll always hate me. I hate myself.'

2. Preeti goes into a toilet cubicle. A group of girls comes in and kicks at the door and then pours coke over the top of the door onto Preeti. When Preeti comes out of the cubicle they trip her up. She says, 'I daren't use the loos any more and I've stopped drinking in school so that I don't have to go. I am so thirsty and have really bad headaches. Yesterday, I fainted in assembly.'

3. Reuben has his bag turned upside down over the toilet bowl. His books, writing equipment and lunch end up in the loo. He says, 'The bullying has got worse and although they threatened me about telling, how do they expect I'm going to explain how my things got soaked? My dad's already suspicious. And this is the third time this week I've had no lunch.'

4. Lydia is fat. Her friends make jokes about her weight. She says, 'I have to laugh with them – they won't think I'm fun if I don't. I feel I am constantly asked to be someone I'm not and at times I feel sickened by it. I don't feel they are good friends but they are the only ones I've got. If I don't behave like they want me to, they'll drop me and I'll be on my own. Recently I've cut down what I eat. I pretend I've had breakfast so that my mum doesn't suspect and at lunchtime I just say I'm not hungry. Getting thin is the only thing that will stop the jokes.'

5. Kendrew frequently trips up, knocks things over and bumps into things. He says, 'I have a problem with co-ordination; friends laugh at me and deliberately try to trip me up to make it worse. One boy hit the underside of my lunch tray – my food and drink went everywhere. Teachers say I'm clumsy and make fun of me and tell me off for dropping books and spilling chemicals. I hate school and I hate everyone in it. I can't wait to leave to have some peace.'

6. Jocasta's friends laugh at her saying, 'No wonder your breath smells eating all that hummus.' Jocasta laughs with them but when she gets home has an argument with her mother about what she is and is not allowed to put in her sandwiches. She won't tell her why. She says, 'I can't help what I eat at home but I don't think they make fun of me about that. I think it's just an excuse to get at me because I'm Greek. And that's something I can't change.'

7. Nathan's bag is grabbed by two boys who run off with it. He says, 'When I found my bag at the end of the school field I saw it was wet. At first I thought they must have emptied a drink bottle over it. Then I realised they'd urinated on it. It all began when I confided to my friend that I thought I was gay. I thought he'd understand. But he told the whole class.'

Friendship skills

The more friends your child has, the more support she has – and the more she learns about other people. Having friends also helps her social skills. It is also important for your child to have a wide number of friends so that if one group doesn't turn out to be nice, she can spend time with another group of friends: children in smaller classes and in smaller schools have fewer opportunities to make alternative friends if they are victimised, which makes it far more likely that they are continuously victimised.

Help your child make friends by asking him to choose one or two other children whom he likes, but has not socialised with much, and invite them home. Invite friends on trips out with your child. Age and development permitting, suggest your child invites friends to go with him bowling, swimming or to the cinema; help with lifts if you don't live close to public transport.

Suggest ways for your child to show care. For example, he could ring up when his friend is off school to find out if he's OK and to keep him up to date with school news. If his friend has been ill, your child could wish him to be better soon. If his friend is off school because someone in the family has died, your child could go over and keep him company, listen to what happened and say how sorry he is. Your child could also try to keep things normal by suggesting they do what they usually do when together.

It is also useful if your child witnesses you being a good friend and hears you say positive things about your friends when they are not around – and to defend them in their absence.

Teachers, especially in primary school, can help your child make friends by pairing her with another child who is likely to be receptive to making friends with her and by giving tasks to do in a team or in pairs. If there is conflict between your child and another child, the teacher could help them settle the argument and repair their friendship.

Discuss friendships with your child

By discussing friendships with your child you will help make him more aware of what to expect from other children and how he can be a better friend himself. It might also encourage him to make friends with children who get left out; shy children are particularly prone to being bullied. Ideas are given below.

Why do we need friends? Suggestions might include: they stop us being lonely, they are people we can have fun with and do things with, they are people who look out for us, they are people who like to do and talk about the things we like to do and talk about, they are people we can tell our secrets to and we can learn from them.

How should we treat our friends? We should smile when we see them and show we are pleased to be with them, be prepared to lend and share things (but must be careful about getting them back), remind them of things they need to do or to avoid, help keep them safe, explain things when they don't understand, help them with their work, comfort them when they are upset, give advice when they are in trouble, look after them when they are ill or hurt – and get help when necessary.

We should allow our friends to have other friends too – friends are not objects to be owned – and we should phone or call at each other's houses in a balanced way so that one of us isn't always doing the work of planning what to do and where to go.

If we see a friend in trouble we should think, 'How would I feel if that were me?' and, 'What would I want someone else to do if this were happening to me?' If a friend is bullying someone else, we can discourage her from taking out her anger on other children. Instead we could show support by listening and finding out why she is upset and why she is behaving like she is. We can help diffuse the situation by using our knowledge of social skills, assertiveness, negotiation and compromise. We can also suggest ways, other than bullying, of helping her feel better.

What should friends not do? We should not gossip, lie or spread rumours about our friends, try to get them into trouble or try to take other friends away from them or shut them out of a friendship group. We must not hurt them in any way and if we are unkind we should apologise after.

We should try not to be jealous of our friends. We should also keep our friends' secrets. However, this final rule should be broken to keep our friends safe – if we know that our friend might harm himself or get hurt by someone else, we must tell. We are not being a good friend if we don't.

Why is it a good idea to have several friends? If we fall out with our best friend, or our best friend leaves the area or is off school sick for a long time, we'll still have other friends to spend time with. Having many friends makes school more enjoyable – especially in secondary school as we have individual timetables and so might be split up from the usual friends we sit with.

Having many friends also allows for a range of interests and in what activities we do – some friends like doing sporty things and others don't. Also, different friends are good at different things. Some might be great fun to be with but not very good at sympathising when things go wrong.

9

HELPING CHILDREN TO MANAGE THEIR ANGER

Children who bully physically may have a great deal of anger stored up inside which makes them want to take out how they feel on someone else. Some victims, especially boys, say that being bullied makes them angry; angry victims are at increased risk of becoming bully/victims. By discussing anger and recognising that it does have its place, your child can become more aware of his feelings and be better able to control them.

Anger: is it good or bad?

Many children think anger is a negative emotion as they so often get into trouble for displaying angry behaviour. However, anger can also be a positive emotion. Ask your child to give examples of when anger can be good, and when it can be bad.

Useful anger is when a parent needs to show a child that she has overstepped the boundary of acceptable behaviour – for, perhaps, the third time. The child didn't listen before so the message has to be given in stronger terms. Anger might also be useful when a parent is angry the first time something happens because what the child did, or was about to do, was very unsafe – here the message needs to be very clear.

Letting off steam is sometimes good – and it can be done so that no one, including the angry person, gets hurt. Sometimes frustration overspills in such a way that the person is overwhelmed. Think of a child whose dog has just been run over and killed. How can he deal with the unfairness of losing his much loved pet? It might do him good to cry and thump his pillow. Later, when he is calm, he might let his parents comfort him; seeing his behaviour told them how much he was hurting inside.

Sometimes anger shows that there is something wrong in the person's life and gives the drive to make a positive change – or to make a complaint about something that was unfair to stop it happening to the person again and, hopefully, to other people.

Destructive anger is when someone loses control to damage something or to hurt someone – including herself. Some children develop eating disorders as a way of dealing with how they feel or they self-harm in a more direct way. Some children maim or even murder other children because of anger – not necessarily because they are angry with the child they attacked but because they find it unbearable to be themselves.

Other angry children might vandalise cars or windows or set fire to things – just because they feel angry and are out of control. Anger can warp the way children see the world and it can become, to them, a hostile and threatening place to be, with no one to trust.

Do children gain from uncontrolled or destructive anger?
Ask your child about uncontrolled anger – is it something that gets a person what he wants? Sometimes people are angry to make a point. But do they actually manage to make that point?

Although it may initially feel good to get rid of the volcano building up inside it doesn't solve whatever the problem is in the long term. The volcano can erupt time and again. And every time there will be consequences. This may mean getting into trouble at home, at school or with the police. It may also mean losing friends. Taking anger out on another person also makes that person feel angry back. Dealing with a situation with aggression increases aggression – and conflict. Hatred will flourish in such situations. This will do nothing to improve how the angry person feels in the long term.

It is hard to say sorry at the best of times but even harder when someone is angry. It is also harder to accept an apology from an angry person – why should someone allow herself to be treated with disrespect? Why should she give the angry person another opportunity to lose control with her at some time in the future?

Being out of control is not something to feel proud of – but learning to use emotions skilfully and productively does earn respect. Discuss the situations below with your child.

Situation 1

A friend has to break an arrangement to meet because he has to take his sister to an after-school club as their mum is ill. You swear at him and stomp away.

Does that tell your friend that you are disappointed he can't make it? No. He will only see your anger, not how you care about having his company.

How could you have handled it? Say, 'That's a shame. I was looking forward to it. Maybe tomorrow?' or, 'Oh. How about tomorrow?' or, 'Why don't I come with you to the after-school club?'

Result? Your friend will know that you understand and that your friendship is strong enough to take setbacks.

Situation 2

You feel that a teacher has behaved unfairly towards you. You storm out of the classroom after kicking over your chair.

Does that tell your teacher that she has been unfair? No. She will think more badly of you than she had done previously.

How could you have handled it? Say, 'I don't think you've been fair with me. I feel you've picked on me all lesson for no good reason. And I tried hard today but you didn't notice that.'

Result? The teacher might think again about what went on in class and might acknowledge that although there had been some improvement she had only noticed the bad. She might treat you more kindly next lesson because you showed she'd upset you and because you told her you had been trying.

Where does the anger come from?
Ask your child why some children have a great deal of anger.

Many children are angry because life has been hard for them, they suffer a big disappointment, they can't cope with what has happened to them, or they are feeling frustrated, trapped or out of control of their lives. They may have low self-esteem and over-react when someone puts them down or they may get aggressive to deal with feeling bad about themselves. Some children have a medical condition that makes them react to situations aggressively.

Children might have witnessed anger between their parents so behave aggressively copying the behaviour they see; they might have experienced their parents' anger directed at them. Suffering can make children want to make other people – or animals – suffer too. Sometimes children see someone behave in an angry way in a certain situation then when they find themselves in a similar situation they model how the first person reacted.

Many children feel unable to talk about their feelings or share them with other people. Their feelings can get bottled up so that, when they can't take any more, they let them out in a destructive explosion of anger.

How to bring anger under control
Ask your child what things she might do to help her control her anger. Some suggestions are given below.

Practical tips include: deliberately relax your muscles, slow your breathing, count to twenty, hold your breath after breathing out and bite your lip – before responding verbally. Or 'wait until you've slept on it' before replying to an email that's upset you. Have a mantra to repeat such as, 'I will not let this person get the better of me. I will stay calm.'

Recall angry occasions when nothing positive was gained. Did those situations really warrant such a response? Did it matter? Does it matter now? Shouldn't you let it go? Were you being reasonable by behaving like that? You want to be dealt with fairly – had you dealt with the other person fairly?

Deal with your anger in a positive way. Tell yourself you have a right to feel angry about what happened – but focus on the problem and the outcome you want to achieve and work on the best way to achieve it.

Reassure yourself that if you work at controlling your anger it will become easier over time.

Try walking away from your anger and instead talk to someone about how you feel.

Ask for support from your friends to remind you to keep control and ask your friends not to provoke you deliberately. Let friends calm you down, encourage you to talk about your problems and discourage reactions using violence.

Allow for bad days when it is very hard to keep control – but by recognising bad days, you can try to avoid any confrontation and warn friends not to tease. Even if someone does tease you, remind yourself that you are playing into that child's hands if you react. If you stop reacting, perhaps that person will leave you alone?

Accept responsibility for what you have done if you lose control of your anger – and accept that there have to be consequences.

Rethink your personal rules – you don't have to take out revenge on everyone who does, or says, something to upset you.

Concentrate on looking for the good in other children, in yourself and in situations.

See vulnerabilities as points of understanding rather than targets.

Celebrate individuality and be prepared to accept imperfection – who wants to look the same, talk the same and have the same thoughts as everyone else?

Conflict, negotiation and compromise

Conflict arises when two or more children want the same thing – or have opposite viewpoints. It can lead to aggression if neither side is prepared to budge but then neither side 'wins' as each fights his own ground. Children who fight to get what they want at the expense of other children are bullies – the bullies are seen to 'win' and the other children to 'lose'. With negotiation and compromise, it is possible for both sides to 'win' and then the situation is considered fair.

Clearly some situations, such as home and school rules are non-negotable. But it is hard to advocate conflict resolution either at home or in school if children witness or experience adults behaving in a way that is all out to win.

Negotiation is usually about making deals with people: 'If I do this, will you do that?' and diffusing any anger that someone might have when they are in conflict. This can be done by staying calm and showing the other person that you understand his point of view.

Compromise is all about achieving an outcome that is somewhere between the extremes hoped for by the two parties involved. Negotiating to reach an acceptable compromise needs to be taught at home and at school. Children need to see their parents managing to come to an agreement on a point of conflict and they need to see that children can negotiate with their teachers – allowing homework to be handed in late, for example, when a child needs to go away for two days to attend a funeral.

Encourage negotiation with your child – either initiated by him or by you – and soon he will learn that he can successfully negotiate to achieve an outcome that is acceptable to him and you, and he may take his skills to school to use with friends.

Work through the following tasks with your child. Then role play the situations to give him confidence to diffuse conflict and to negotiate in situations that arise in his own life.

Task 1

Jo wants to go to a party and asks her parents to take her there. But they have arranged to go out to the cinema and they won't be back in time.

What might Jo and her parents agree on? Jo wants to have fun and her parents want her to enjoy her free time too.

What could Jo suggest as a compromise? Jo could arrange

a lift to the party with a friend and ask if her parents could bring her and that friend home from the party after they've been to the cinema.

Task 2
Chigozie and Oliver have all of Saturday together. Chigozie wants to play football in the park near his house. Oliver wants to go swimming at the new pool that's opened.

What might Chigozie and Oliver agree on? The boys want to spend their Saturday together and they want it to be fun and sporty.

What could the boys suggest as a compromise? They could suggest they go bowling or call on other friends instead – then neither of them gets to do his first choice. Or they could divide their time together, swimming in the morning before the pool gets busy and playing football in the afternoon.

Task 3
Chelsea wants to watch a programme that ends later than her usual bedtime but her parents say no. Chelsea is very upset and angry because she knows that all her friends will be talking about it at school the next day and she'll be the only one not to have seen it.

What should the parents do first? Try to diffuse the situation by calming Chelsea down. They should thank Chelsea for explaining why watching the programme is important to her as now they understand why they can't just record the programme for her to watch after school the next evening.

What might Chelsea and her parents agree on? Chelsea wants to feel happy and her parents want her to feel happy – where they differ is the concern Chelsea's parents have over her being too tired in school if she stays up until the end of the programme. So Chelsea's parents could say, 'Let's try to work out what we can do about it.'

What could Chelsea suggest as a compromise? Chelsea could watch half of the programme before she goes to bed. Then her parents could record the second half. If Chelsea can manage to get up early the next morning she could watch the rest of the programme once she's ready for school. If she doesn't manage to see the second half before school, she can still join in with some of the chat with her friends.

10

TEACHING CHILDREN ASSERTIVENESS SKILLS

If the activities in this chapter are being carried out in schools, children should be grouped with others who have exhibited the same type of behaviour: aggressive children should not be taught assertiveness with passive children as this might intimidate the passive children and encourage the aggressive children to continue intimidating them. Bully/victims will need to have knowledge of how to curb their aggression in some circumstances and how to become less passive in others as they have had experience of bullying and of being bullied. So the whole of this chapter is relevant to them.

Types of behaviour

Behaviour can be considered to be of three main types: aggressive, passive and assertive. Can your child describe behaviours in these categories and say which category best describes her own behaviour? By increasing your child's awareness of these categories, she becomes primed to identify and rectify extremes of her own behaviour – and someone else's.

Aggressive behaviour includes deliberately hurting someone or making him feel small by, for example, calling him lazy or stupid; showing inappropriate angry behaviour; and threatening: 'If you don't . . . I'll . . .'

Passive-aggression is sneaky aggressive behaviour often favoured by relational bullies (bullies who operate to harm relationships). It includes being intolerant of viewpoints other than your own; controlling – making other children do as you ask; begrudging compliments: 'I suppose, for you, it's good'; being tactless: 'I hear your Grandpa's died. Leave you any dosh?'; being manipulative – pretending to like someone because you want something from him; moralising: 'I'd never have done anything like that'; sabotaging – your friend's artwork or splitting up two friends; being sarcastic – saying: 'The boys will love that outfit,' and then pretending to put a finger down your throat; shunning – isolating or ignoring someone; and spreading gossip.

Bullying behaviour is aggressive behaviour. Children who have bullied can be taught how to change aggressive body language to confident body language and how to change aggressive behaviour into assertive behaviour.

Passive behaviour includes allowing things to be said about you or done to you without effectively protecting yourself, saying sorry when something is not your fault, and being unable to state your needs.

Victim behaviour is passive behaviour. Children who have been bullied can be taught how to change passive body language to confident body language and how to change passive behaviour into assertive behaviour.

Assertive behaviour includes showing respect for the other person and explaining needs and feelings clearly without putting someone else down. If children need to criticise someone they do it in a useful or tactful way: 'It might look better like this,' or, 'I've heard that pink and brown don't go.' Assertive children are also able to give genuine and rewarding compliments such as, 'Wow that really suits you.'

Children who are assertive are admired for their fairness, respected for their individuality and for the fact that they don't let others get the better of them. They don't lose control over their emotions; they stay cool, and they accept responsibility for what they do. They know how to behave to reduce conflict, understand that sharing feelings helps them, and they respect other children's rights and defend their own. They also accept themselves as they are, believe in themselves and are not shy of asking for help when it's needed.

Understanding body language

If your child is passive, ask how he thinks other children identify him as a potential victim, even when those children don't know him. Perhaps he had been accidentally tripped up and apologised when it was clearly not his fault or perhaps it's the way he talks, walks, stands and sits? Can he identify passive body language?

If your child is aggressive, can he identify aggressive body language? Can your child suggest how an assertive child might behave? Although assertive children do behave in a confident manner, so do bullies – so what's the difference? Assertive behaviour is non-threatening and serves only to show other people they have the confidence to protect themselves, not to attack.

Aggressive body language includes having hands on hips, leaning threateningly towards someone, scowling, frowning, sneering and making threatening gestures, having arms folded confidently and eyes appearing alert and interested as though looking for 'prey', or glaring or having slitted lids. Speech is loud – perhaps shouting – and can be blaming or threatening.

Passive body language includes lowering of the gaze, being unable to meet the other person's eyes, shuffling of feet and having hunched shoulders, the head bowed and arms folded protectively. Speech is hurried, mumbled, hesitant, stammering or repeatedly tripping on words.

Assertive – or confident – body language includes standing or sitting up straight, when standing having feet slightly apart and the body weight evenly balanced, having shoulders relaxed, being able to meet the other person's eyes, having arms loose either side of the body or in another relaxed position, smiling, having eyes appearing alert and interested in what's going on around – just for pleasure. Speech is calm and clearly understood, sounding smooth.

Protecting victims

When responding verbally to a bully, your child should not start any sentences with 'You . . .' as this is aggressive and may inflame the situation. So, instead of saying, for example, 'You won't get away with this . . .' or, 'You can't do that to me,' or, 'You'll regret this,' your child could say, 'I won't let this go without reporting it,' and, 'If you hurt me in any way I shall tell my parents/a teacher,' and, 'Think again – there will be consequences.' And, of course, once said your child must make sure all these things happen so that the bully takes her seriously.

If your child wants to address something a bully has done, he should not say, 'You're unkind,' as it is not the person who is unkind but his behaviour. Instead he could say, 'What you have done/said is unkind,' or, 'What you have said is racist. I'm surprised you want to show up your prejudice.'

Secondary schoolchildren might feel comfortable adding to this: ' . . and I don't respect you for it.' Primary schoolchildren might like to show that the unkind behaviour is only a part of the child who has been unkind: 'I don't like it when you're mean; I like it when you're kind.' This shows the bullying child that there is an alternative way to behave.

If your child has to address verbal bullying – physical bullying should be tackled by adults as your child is in immediate danger – he should think carefully about what he should and shouldn't say and then practise what he wants to say.

Task 1

Ask your child to think of an occasion when she behaved passively. What happened? Who said what? Who did what? What could she have said or done to behave assertively at that time?

Task 2

Ask your child to write down unkind things said to him and work out what he could have said to stand up for himself. This helps him be ready with a reply if the same thing is said in the future. It can be fun if children work out their responses together in a group. However, they must be assertive responses – aggressive comments increase conflict and victims will then be exhibiting behaviour they have criticised others for. Some ideas are given below but the exact comments needn't be used – your child could think up ones that suit him and the situation better; it is important that he feels comfortable in his new role.

Useful strategies for victims to use
The strategies below could be practised in role play to ensure that your child's body language matches what he says. The bully's comments are given in normal type; the suggested victim's responses are given in italics.

Agree with the bully
'You're so fat.'
'Yes. It's all the doughnuts I eat.'

'You stink of garlic.'
'I would do. We ate loads last night.'

'I could kill you.'
'You could.'

'I heard your dad doesn't work.'
'I heard that too.'

'My Dad says Travellers are the scum of the earth.'
'My Dad says lots of things too.'
'Such as?'
'How some people like to put labels on other people. It makes them feel good.'

Make a joke
'You think you're God's gift to men.'
'Actually, I think they're God's gift to me.'

Bully follows threateningly:
'Do you fancy me? Is that why you follow me around?'
'You're dead.'
Looks around in amazement. 'Well, you're here with me so you must be too. Nice of you to keep me company; shall we share funerals?'

'You're stupid.'
'Are you offering to coach me?'

'Go to hell.'
'Will you show me the way?'

'Your ears stick out.'
'They help me hear better,' or, *'I was an elephant in a previous life.'*

'You're weird.'
'It runs in the family.'

'Carrot top.'
'It helps cannibals see in the dark.'

Deflect insults
'I've never seen so many spots on a face.'
'That's because I'm kind and welcoming,' or, *'Looks aren't everything.'*

'You're the ugliest person I've ever seen.'
'Yet you can't stop looking at me. There must be some attraction for you.'

'You're stupid.'
'But I've got a kind heart.'

'You're a freak!'
'It's OK to be different.'

'I could kill you.'
'But then you'd miss me.'
'In your dreams.'
'I'm sorry to disappoint you but I don't dream about you.'

Ask questions
Bully says nasty things.
'Are you jealous of me? Is that why you pick on me?' or, *'Are you hoping for a career in acting?'*
'What are you on about?'
'Well, you want to be centre stage all the time.'

'You're scum!'
'Has someone said that to you? Is that why you're saying it to me?'

'You're a slag.'
'Slag means lots of things. Which definition are you referring to?'

'Your parents are ancient; they'll be fossils by the time you're grown up.'
'Any particular kind?'

Make the bully feel uncomfortable
Bully (boy) deliberately rubs past a girl.
'Do you get an erection when you rub past me like that?'

'Are you still a virgin? Bet you are.'
'Why do you want to know? Because you wish you had some of it or because you want to know what it's like?'

General remarks can include:
'People who bully are usually bullied themselves. Who's bullied you?'

'It's a shame you don't put your energy into something more positive.'

'I take it you don't want the school to give you a good reference when you leave. Are you hoping to claim benefits instead of working?'

'Would you be as brave without your friends to back you up?'

'The odds are stacked in your favour. Are you a coward?'

'Do you have such little control over your temper that it overspills at the slightest thing?'

'I wonder what you'll be in your next life to pay for all your nasty behaviour.'

'Did you know bullying is bad for your mental and physical health? If you like, I'll come with you to the Head of Year to get you the help you need.'

'Are you having a bad day? Is that why you're taking it out on me?'

'What's gone wrong at home for you to behave like this?'

Mention feelings

'Your mum can't walk. I saw her in a wheelchair.'
'I'm so proud of all she does. I am sure if your mum couldn't walk, you'd be proud of her too.'

General remarks can include:
'Does being a bully make you feel proud of yourself?'

'I thought you were my friend so why do you want to hurt my feelings?'

'Is that how you get your kicks? By being nasty to people?'

'Are you jealous of me? . . . Then why spend so much time trying to hurt me?'

'I'm sure you don't really want to hurt me – you're just hurting inside and so you're taking it out on me.'

'Does it make you feel big picking on someone smaller than you?'

'We used to be such good friends. I don't deserve this from you.'

Deliberately misunderstand

'You think you're so clever.'
'Well I wasn't sure; thanks for boosting my self-esteem,' or, *'Perhaps I am.'*

'Smart a***.'
'Gosh. Thanks.'

'Fat cow.'
'Thanks for noticing.'

Be sympathetic

Bully says something nasty.

'Oh, I expect you're having a bad day. Want to talk about it?' or, *'Do you have a problem? Would you like to share it with me?'*
'You're my only problem.'
'Really? Shall we talk about it so that we can make up? Having bad feelings between people is not good, don't you agree?'

Be direct

In Chapter 3, *To punish or not to punish*? Bethany was bullying Amber by isolating her from friends and preventing her from going to the after-school club. But Georgina stood up to Bethany: 'I will play with Amber if I want. You can't stop me. And you can't stop me from going to the after-school club either.' Bethany left Georgina alone and didn't try to stop her from playing with Amber or from going to the after-school club.

Other general direct comments include:

'Stop being nasty to me.'

'I don't like the way you are talking to me. Stop it.'

'If you can't be polite to me there's no point in continuing the conversation.'

Point out unkind behaviour

This is particularly useful for children in primary schools who may not be able to think up witty or challenging responses. Children find it much easier to react with how they feel or what they have been told.

'You're a w****r.'
'That was a horrible thing to say.'

'No, you can't play with us.'
'Do you like having friends? . . . I do too.'

Bully shoves into another boy.
'Hey, it's rude to push. If you want to get by, ask nicely.'

'You can't have these. I'm playing with them.'
'Mr A says it's selfish not to share.'

Say no

'Give me your dinner money.'
'No.'

'Come with us to the park after school – if you dare.'
'No. I don't want to.'

Responding to racist bullying
'Black w****r.'
*'Does that make you a white w****r?'*

'Rubber lips!'
'Haven't you heard that black guys are great kissers?' or,
'Well, I'll certainly never need implants.'

'Your hair's so bad you have to cover it up.'
'Actually I'm hiding the beauty of it so that you won't suffer from jealousy.'

'I don't play with black children.'
'Why not?'

'Paki.'
'Why do you think that everyone who's Asian is from Pakistan?'

Responding to homophobic bullying
Boys bullying boys
'Get out of our changing rooms – I'm not your cheap thrill.'
'Don't worry. You're not my type.'

'You're such a wuss.'
'Could you spell that so I can look it up?'

'You're a big girl's blouse.'
'Perhaps I should find a big girl to wear me then,' or, *'That sounds nice, snuggling up to a big girl.'*

'Keep away from me you poof.'
'I've heard that people who are homophobic deep down aren't confident about their own sexuality.'

'You're a pansy.'
'I've always liked the colour purple.'

Girls bullying girls
'You're so butch you look like a bloke.'
'Good. I like men.'

'Get away from me. Hey, she's trying to jump me.'
'Starring in your own drama? Don't you know that lesbians don't just fancy anyone? They have to be special.'

Responding to teachers
It is very hard for children to challenge teachers – only the most confident or desperate might feel able to do it. But if they can, there are some suggestions below. If the teacher did not intend any harm this would be sufficient to make him stop or rethink his behaviour. If this is not possible for your child to do, then either you should phone the school and make an appointment to discuss it with the Headteacher or Head of Year or you should ask your child to take the problem to a teacher she trusts.

When the issue affects more than one child, a group of children could complain to someone higher in authority. In Carlotta's school, a male teacher was giving the class lessons on sex education as part of the science curriculum. Mr B kept mentioning eggs and bacon when referring to girls' ovaries producing eggs and the boys in the class were joining Mr B in laughing about it. This made the girls feel very unhappy and vulnerable and a group of them complained to another teacher. The complaint was looked into, together with a number of other complaints. Since the teacher had previously been disciplined, Mr B was dismissed.

General remarks include:

'Please let me explain. I think there's been a misunderstanding.'

'You're right, I am late but there is a good reason. Can I tell you?'

'Please could you tell me where I went wrong as I don't understand why my marks are so low.'

'I have tried very hard this week but I still seem to get into trouble just as much. I feel you're picking on me.'

'I don't feel comfortable listening to personal remarks,' or, *'I don't think teachers should say things like that about their pupils.'*

Reducing aggression in bullies

Children who bully do not need help in standing up for themselves – although they need to learn to do that in non-aggressive ways. They need to practise positive behaviour to help them be more connected to other people fostering mutual liking, understanding and respect – as well as empathy.

Task 1

Ask your child to think of an occasion when he has behaved aggressively towards someone. What happened? Who said what? Who did what? What could he have said or done to behave assertively at that time?

Task 2

Children with aggression find it hard to compliment other people or to look for the good in people. Ask your child to think up three things she likes about each of her friends, siblings – or you – and tell them. And your child should try to compliment – in a genuine way – at least one person a day. What can she compliment herself about? Say what you admire in your child. Think of as many things as you can – and keep them genuine.

Task 3

Children with aggression find it hard to ask for help – and then to thank graciously the person who gave it afterwards. Challenge your child to go into shops to ask if they sell something and to ask where to find a particular item – and show gratitude afterwards.

Task 4

Children with aggression find it difficult to work as a team. Ask your child to perform a task with friends, with siblings or with you. Think of something that is worthwhile such as a project to rescue a wild garden. The end goal might be to make the garden attractive and pleasing to spend time in or to grow vegetables or herbs.

Or the task could be simply to plan, shop for and cook a meal together. Or you might want to swap rooms around in the house – you will all have to work co-operatively to ensure that the operation runs smoothly and you will need to discuss and value everyone's contribution as how to fulfil the task best.

Or you might want to redecorate your child's bedroom. Visit DIY shops to choose paints with your child. You could visit car boot sales, jumble sales, charity shops or check in the free ad newspapers for curtains that will match the preferred colour scheme if buying them new is not feasible – or to help your child appreciate working to a budget to help him understand the value of money. Some children are given plenty of money too easily, freely spend it and then demand more.

There is also the 'freecycle' scheme that has been set up to help reduce landfills. Look on the Internet to find your local freecycle site. Once you've joined your local group you can post a request for the particular furnishings your child would like and, with luck, might receive them for free.

Task 5

Encourage your child to keep a diary of how often she has displayed prosocial behaviour in the categories below – and some others!

Admit feelings
Target: 'Hey, do you like my new jeans? They're designer.'
Don't say, *'You like to rub it in don't you?'*
Say, *'They're great. I feel envious because I can't afford any like that.'*

Show sympathy
Target: Is crying.
Don't say, *'What a cry baby!'*
Say, *'What's up? Can I help?'*

Apologise for past behaviour
Target: 'Please don't hurt me again.'
Don't say, *'Why should today be any different from all the other days?'*
Say, *'I won't. I'm sorry. It's over.'*

Give compliments
Target: Has a spotty face.
Don't say, *'What have you been doing to cultivate such a crop?'*
Say, *'I like your hair today,' or, 'I thought the goal you saved last week was good.'*

Connect with other people
Target: Listening to music.
Don't say, *'What crap are you listening to?'*
Say, *'What kind of music do you like? Rap music? That's cool.'*

Target: 'My rabbit died last night.'
Don't say, *'Get over it.'*
Say, *'I'm sorry. I was sad when my dog died.'*

Empowering bystanders

Bystanders too can take advantage of assertiveness training to make it easier to intervene when they see bullying behaviour. Children who have learnt assertiveness skills can also empower other children – bullies can't operate if others don't collude with their behaviour.

Ask your child what he would do in the following situations. He could role play each situation after discussing what to do. He must behave assertively and should not slip into aggression.

Task 1

Two boys go up to a boy in the schoolyard and say, sniggering, 'Hey, Ezekiel, Mandy says she wants to go out with you. Will you go out with her?' You know that Mandy would have no interest in going out with Ezekiel and that the boys are teasing him. What would you do?

Suggestion: Go up to Ezekiel and say, 'They know Mandy doesn't want to go out with you,' and, to the boys, 'Leave him alone. What's he done to you?'

Task 2

A group of girls is playing a game. One of them is much bigger than the rest and there is one girl who is much smaller than the rest. The biggest girl keeps shoving the smallest girl until the smallest girl says, 'Stop pushing me. I don't like it when you do that.' The biggest girl then starts pushing all the other girls and says, 'See. I'm not just doing it to you I'm doing it to everyone. Why are you making such a fuss about it?' What would you do?

Suggestion: Say, 'I saw you push that girl around and now you're pushing us all around. That's bullying. Stop it now and apologise or I'll get the teacher.'

Task 3

Ask your child to think of occasions when she had witnessed bullying. What happened? What did she do? What could she have said and done?

Motivating children to change their behaviour

Some children are resistant to, or ambivalent about (in two minds), changing their behaviour. For change to occur children need to have high self-esteem or they won't see a point to changing, they need to recognise their behaviour as unhelpful and have strategies to make the changes. They also need to be able to identify personal concerns over their behaviour, recognise the disadvantages of carrying on without change and believe that they have the ability to change. If your child is reluctant to change, ensure any discussion you have with him is non-judgmental.

Eliciting a need to change from passive children

Recognise their behaviour as unhelpful. Ask your child, 'What have you gained from being passive? What have you lost from being passive? How do you see your life when you leave school? What do you hope to do? What other ambitions do you have when you are adult? Is your current behaviour going to help you achieve them?'

'How do you think friends/parents/siblings/teachers see you? How would you like them to view you? Is your current behaviour going to help you achieve that?'

Recognise the disadvantages of carrying on without change. If your child continues passive behaviour, does she realise that she is likely to be continued to be taken advantage of? If not now, then some time in the future? Timid children are easily identified and she would be at risk of victimisation in the future – at school, at further education or at work.

Identify personal concerns over their behaviour. Passive behaviour is not going to keep your child safe; she must be feeling unhappy and scared – and may be angry or humiliated. Changing her behaviour can make her feel happier and more confident.

Believe that they have the ability to change. If your child says she'd like to change, why is that? And why hasn't she already? What's stopping her? How can she make it easier for herself to change? She might, for example, want to start practising being assertive with family members first, to gain the confidence to use the techniques in school. She might need to ask her friends to stop asking teachers for things on her behalf as she needs to practise seeing to her own needs. Is there anyone your child particularly admires for dealing with situations in assertive ways? Could she use that person as her role model?

To help passive children appraise their progress they need to have clear signs to look out for. Ask, 'How will you know that your behaviour is becoming less passive?' If your child doesn't know how to answer, try asking, 'How do people behave towards you now? How do you think this might change?'

Initially your child might have only one or two suggestions. But if this question is repeated after she has started to be more assertive, she may notice many more things. Asking the question in the first place sharpens children's observational skills and makes them more aware of the effect their behaviour has on other people.

Changes she might see in how other people relate to her might include: 'I get bullied less; my friends listen more to what I say; friends take more notice of ideas I have; teachers don't have to keep asking me to repeat what I say – they hear me the first time; more children have acted in a friendly way towards me; teachers have given me more responsibility and my desire to protect myself has increased. You have said how proud you are of me.'

Eliciting a need to change from aggressive children

Recognise their behaviour as unhelpful. Ask your child, 'What have you gained from being aggressive? What have you lost from being aggressive? Where do you see your life leading when you leave school? Is the behaviour you have shown in school likely to help you get what you want as an adult?'

Recognise the disadvantages of carrying on without change. If your child wants to continue aggressive behaviour, does he realise that the school cannot give him a positive reference for work and that he is at risk of being excluded? How might this affect his education? What kind of job is he hoping for? If he can't get on with other people now, how will that affect how he can get on with other people in the future? What about the need to get on with a life partner? And with children? What kind of role model is he likely to be for his own children?

Ask, 'How do you think friends/parents/siblings/teachers see you? How would you like them to view you? Is your current behaviour going to help achieve that?'

Identify personal concerns over their behaviour. If your child bullies in a physical way, does he realise that he is at greater risk of becoming a criminal than children who don't bully? Is that a future to be desired? Does he worry about his behaviour? Is it getting out of control?

Believe that they have the ability to change. If your child says he'd like to change, why is that? And why hasn't he already? What's stopping him? How could he make it easier for himself to change? This might, for example, involve changing friendship groups or making new friends who don't encourage aggressive behaviour. However, it is hard to change if a child is the only one of the group who wants to change. So an alternative option would be to invite all group members to change with your child. Is there anyone your child particularly admires for dealing with situations in non-aggressive ways? Could he use that person as his role model?

To help aggressive children appraise their progress they need to have clear signs to look out for. Ask, 'How will you know that your behaviour is becoming less aggressive?' If your child doesn't know how to answer, try asking, 'How do people behave towards you now? How do you think this might change if you stop being aggressive?'

As mentioned above, your child may notice more signs over time and they might include: 'I notice more people smiling at me; I got praised for something; I don't get told off as much; other children don't look so scared of me; other children don't avoid me as much; my desire to bully has lessened; I've been given more responsibility and people show they trust me more. You have said how proud you are of me.'

SUMMARY

A great deal of advice has been given in this book so it is useful to summarise the main points here. It is important to note that to stop bullying everyone needs to pull together: schools and their staff, parents of all children, victims and other schoolchildren.

What schools can do to stop bullying

- Have strong leadership and a strong anti-bullying policy that reflects current trends in bullying behaviours found in, and outside of, the school.
- Ensure all staff members are aware of their role in tackling bullying and that they deal with bullying in a consistent way.
- Have some staff trained to deal specifically with bullying issues.
- Ensure there is sufficient staff supervision at break times and lunch times and at the start and end of school days, and have a supervised 'safe' room for vulnerable children to go to.
- Inform parents how they can help stop bullying and involve parents when bullying has been reported.
- Have several strategies to choose from when tackling a bullying situation and always follow up to check that bullying has stopped. The priority must always be on keeping the victim safe.
- Make bullying and related issues such as racism and sexuality part of the curriculum and openly value minority groups. Ask

staff members to consider carefully the language they use.
- Ban camera phones and have class discussions on the appropriate use of mobile phones and the internet.
- Make school a rewarding place to be by valuing individuals and taking special care of children who are challenged in any way.
- Introduce a peer support system in school if the school does not already have one and train older pupils to help younger pupils with particular difficulties.

What teachers can do to stop bullying
- Have clear classroom rules and sanctions and praise children who remain within the boundaries of the rules and who demonstrate prosocial behaviour.
- Promote prosocial behaviour by example and by showing expectations of prosocial behaviour in pupils such as co-operation, compromise and friendliness.
- Show care to children and expect them to show care to others too to increase connectedness between you. Emphasise commonalities.
- Intervene before a situation has time to escalate and discuss what happened and why with the children involved. Help provide children with solutions to resolve their difficulties.
- Avoid prejudicial and stereotypical comments. Try to value everyone in the class and avoid favouritism.
- Always deal respectfully and fairly towards children.
- Discuss bullying issues in class and explain the vital role of the bystander and how early intervention can stop bullying.
- Encourage children to tell about bullying and always act on information given while respecting the wishes of the person who gave it to you.

What parents can do to stop bullying
- Tell your child how much you love her and be physically affectionate. Children need to know that they are loved to feel good about themselves and to know that they are worth defending.
- Try to be around for key points in your child's day such

as when he gets home from school and at breakfast and supper times to show care and to know what is going on in his life.

- Actively listen to what your child says to identify problem areas. Very often much can be gleaned from noting what a child leaves out as well as what she actually says.
- Involve the school and enlist the help of your child's friends with his agreement when there is a problem.
- Help your child to make friends. Talk about what it is that makes someone a good friend and be a good friend to your friends and neighbours. Respect the community around you and take care not to drop litter or allow your child to: otherwise she will get the message that other people don't matter.
- Avoid showing prejudices and making judgmental comments about other people.
- Say how hurt you feel when someone says something to upset you – but be prepared to admit to being in the wrong if another person's comment is justified. This will help your child think carefully about what he says and will help him accept responsibility for what he says and does.
- Accept it when you are told that your child has bullied – don't try to protect her as that will reward her for bullying behaviour.
- She needs to get a clear message that bullying is wrong.
- Teach your child assertiveness skills and social skills – which will also increase his self-confidence and self-esteem. Also explain his personal rights and display them at home – for example, on his bedroom wall or on a kitchen cupboard – and encourage him to defend them.
- Raise empathy in your child so that she is less likely to bully and less likely to ignore bullying of other children. Watch and discuss television programmes with your child, talk about your feelings and encourage your child to express her feelings.
- Teach your child anger management and negotiation skills – and practise them at home. Consider the way you handle anger and whether you would benefit from negotiating issues with family members.

- Keep your child safe. If the school can't stop the bullying, involve the police or temporarily withdraw your child from school and seek advice from a parent support group such as Parentline Plus.

What victims can do to stop bullying

- Always tell an adult and get help from anyone who will listen.
- Get support from those who love you and from helplines.
- Consider a variety of ways to stop the bullying – ignore it, challenge the bully, make jokes or keep telling an adult until he puts a stop to it.
- Keep evidence of bullying and keep a diary of what happened when and who witnessed it.
- Report cyber bullying to mobile phone companies, internet service providers, chat room administrators, etc. Block troublesome phone numbers and email addresses.

What schoolchildren can do to stop bullying

- Stand up for the victim the moment someone acts unfairly towards him – this may prevent the situation escalating into bullying on a regular basis.
- Intervene to stop the bully from hurting the victim – if the situation is too much for you to handle alone, get help. If you and your friends don't collude with the bully, she will stop.
- Give emotional support to the victim and befriend him.
- Always tell an adult about what has happened to keep the victim safe.
- Calm down an angry friend and encourage her to talk about her feelings and to deal with anger and hurt in useful ways rather than destructive ways such as by taking it out on another child.

By everyone acting together to stop bullying, children will be able to concentrate on what's really important in life: humanity and achieving their personal potential.

INDEX

125

To order any Right Way title please fill in the form below

No. of copies	Title	Price	Total
	How to be a People Person	£5.99	
	Take Charge of Your Future	£5.99	
	For P&P add £2.50 for the first book, £1 for each additional book		
	Grand Total		£

Name: _____

Address:_____

_____ Postcode: _____

Daytime Tel. No./Email _____
(in case of query)

Three ways to pay:
1. Telephone the TBS order line on 01206 255 800.
   Order lines are open Monday – Friday, 8:30am–5:30pm.
2. I enclose a cheque made payable to **TBS Ltd** for £_____
3. Please charge my ☐ Visa ☐ Mastercard ☐ Amex
   ☐ Maestro (issue no. _____)

Card number:_____

Expiry date: _____ Last three digits on back of card:_____

Signature: _____
(your signature is essential when paying by credit or debit card)

**Please return forms to Cash Sales/Direct Mail Dept.,
The Book Service, Colchester Road, Frating Green,
Colchester CO7 7DW.**

Enquiries to readers@constablerobinson.com.

Constable and Robinson Ltd (directly or via its agents)
may mail, email or phone you about promotions or products.

☐ Tick box if you do not want these from us ☐ or our subsidiaries.

**www.right-way.co.uk
www.constablerobinson.com**